WRESTLING

WRESTLING
Skills and Strategies for the Athlete and Coach

John Johnston
Coach of Wrestling
at Princeton University

and

Chet Dalgewicz
Assistant Coach of Wrestling
at Princeton University

with

Dan White

Photographs by James Whittier Parker

HAWTHORN BOOKS, INC.
Publishers/New York
A Howard & Wyndham Company

WRESTLING: SKILLS AND STRATEGIES FOR THE ATHLETE AND COACH

Copyright © 1979 by John Johnston, Chet Dalgewicz, and Dan White. Copyright under International and Pan-American Copyright Conventions. All rights reserved, including the right to reproduce this book or portions thereof in any form, except for the inclusion of brief quotations in a review. All inquiries should be addressed to Hawthorn Books, Inc., 260 Madison Avenue, New York, New York 10016. This book was manufactured in the United States of America and published simultaneously in Canada by Prentice-Hall of Canada, Limited, 1870 Birchmount Road, Scarborough, Ontario.

Library of Congress Catalog Card Number: 78-61578
ISBN: 0-8015-8933-9
  3 4 5 6 7 8 9 10

We offer this book as a token of our esteem for the many wrestlers we have been privileged to coach during our careers.

Contents

	Introduction	xi
	General Information about Wrestling	3
1	Takedowns	5
	Stance 5	
	Set-Up 9	
	Penetration 11	
	Finish-Off 14	
	Lower Body Takedown Maneuvers 14	
	Upper Body Takedown Maneuvers 20	
	Combined Upper-Lower Body Takedown Maneuvers 31	
	Takedowns from Kneeling-Facing 61	
2	Offensive Moves from the Bottom	62
	Base Positions 62	
	Escapes 64	
	Reversals 79	
3	Control and Pinning Combinations	91
	Control 91	
	Riding Maneuvers 92	
	Pinning Combinations 104	
	Control and Pinning Situations Using the Legs 118	
4	General Defensive Positions	124
	Lines of Defense 124	
	Defensing Neutral Position Attacks 125	
	Countering Upper Body Attacks 131	
	Defensing Bottom Offense 132	
	Defensing Top Offense 140	
	Pinning Defense 146	
5	Becoming a Good Wrestler	149
	Setting Goals 150	

　　　　　Practice　151
　　　　　Skill Development　152
　　　　　Daily Practice Schedule　153
　　　　　A Weekly Practice Schedule　154
　　　　　Conditioning　155

6　Skill Improvement Drills　　　　　　　　　　　　　　157
　　　　　Neutral Position　157
　　　　　Bottom　158
　　　　　Top　160
　　　　　Mat Drills　160

7　Weight-Training Exercises　　　　　　　　　　　　　162
　　　　　Conventional Weight-Training
　　　　　　Exercises　162
　　　Universal Weight Program　163

Appendix: Instructions for a Match　　　　　　　　　　165

Glossary　　　　　　　　　　　　　　　　　　　　　　　167

Index　　　　　　　　　　　　　　　　　　　　　　　　172

Acknowledgments

We wish to thank Chris McKinley and Emily Bennett for their invaluable assistance in the preparation of this manuscript; and Kirk Dabney, Dave Trombadore, Keith Ely, and Glen Ely—all Princeton wrestlers who posed for the photographs.

Introduction

This is a textbook about wrestling for both the beginner and the experienced wrestler, and for both the fan and the coach. Our purpose is to pass on to those who love this great sport some of the knowledge we have gained in our many years of experience as competitors and as coaches.

The temptation in such an endeavor is to try to tell all. But, just as coaches must when organizing their practices, we have exercised considerable restraint and confined ourselves to talking about what we think can best help.

We urge you to use this as a textbook. Consult its index whenever you want to refresh your memory on a particular point. The beginning wrestler will find here all the techniques he needs to start his career. The sophisticated wrestler can take from these pages certain refinements that will help him continue to improve.

Fans of wrestling will enjoy studying the strategy and reading the language of wrestling.

And the coach will find helpful ideas on such subjects as practice organization, drills, strategy, techniques, weight loss, and so on.

There is something here for everyone. Our fascination with this ancient sport is based in part on its youthful demeanor. By that apparent contradiction, we mean that wrestling—despite its venerable age—continues to evolve, to change, to improve its potential for drama and excitement, to raise even higher its standards of grace and strength and courage. If you sense our enthusiasm and love for the sport, and find in this book some helpful ideas, then we have succeeded.

WRESTLING

General Information about Wrestling

When two opponents wrestle, one tries to defeat the other by pinning the back of both shoulders to the mat for one second in college contests, two seconds in high school. If neither wrestler pins the other, the winner is determined by a point system.

There are five ways to score points. If one wrestler takes down his opponent, he is awarded 2 points. If he escapes the hold of his opponent, he gains 1 point. If he escapes the hold and establishes his own control of his foe in what is known as a reversal, he receives 2 points.

If a wrestler pins one of his opponent's shoulders to the mat and holds the other shoulder close to the mat, but not touching, and at an angle of less that 45 degrees, for a period of less than 5 seconds, he has accomplished a near fall worth 2 points. A 3-point near fall is like the 2-point version, except that the offensive man holds the raised shoulder of his adversary at an angle of less than 45 degrees for more than 5 seconds.

In college wrestling, the offensive wrestler receives 1 point if he controls or rides his opponent a net time of at least 1 minute.

Penalty points also can be awarded for technical violations such as stalling and for illegal holds such as bending a limb beyond the normal limit of its movement, strangle holds, head scissors, and so forth.

All matches occur on a soft protective mat inside a circle with a minimum diameter of 28 feet. A smaller circle 10 feet in diameter is marked at the center of the mat and serves as the starting point for action.

Matches last 6 minutes in high school, 8 minutes in college. High school matches are divided into three 2-minute periods, college bouts into a 2–3–3 pattern. There are no intervals of rest between periods.

The first period is always begun with the two wrestlers standing and facing each other at the center of the mat, arms not locked or touching.

In the final 2 periods, both wrestlers assume a referee's position in which one wrestler is on the bottom, the other on top. Each reverses his position at the start of the third period.

Wrestling techniques involve lifting, throwing, twisting, tackling, and tripping. In some respects, wrestling is a science, for most maneuvers employ the principle of leverage. There are hundreds of holds and maneuvers but no wrestler should try to master every one. Rather, he should learn and perfect those that best suit his body build. It is better to be expert at a few holds than mediocre at a great many. You should study all the available techniques for your maneuvers so that you can be certain you are employing the best available methods.

Great strength is an asset but not a prerequisite in wrestling. Knowledge of leverage points, quickness, and physical conditioning are far more essential to success.

There are various weight classifications that allow athletes, regardless of their size, to participate against opponents who are approximately the same weight. In high school, there are 12 recommended pound-weight categories: 98, 105, 112, 119, 126, 132, 138, 145, 155, 167, 185, and unlimited. In college, the classes are 118, 126, 134, 142, 150, 158, 167, 177, 190, and unlimited.

It needs to be said that wrestling is a sport for individuals. A coach can yell encouragement and tips on strategy from the sideline, but once the wrestler is on the mat he must rely on his own skills and judgment.

1

Takedowns

The *takedown* is a single maneuver or a series of maneuvers by which a wrestler in a neutral position takes his opponent to the mat and gains control over him. The takedown is the most highly skilled technique in modern wrestling and requires more practice than any other aspect of the sport.

A takedown has three components: the set-up, the maneuver, and the finish-off. If you are a beginning wrestler, you will probably become quickly adept at taking your man to the mat, but you will have to learn from experience and constant practice how to properly set him up and finish him off. Good wrestlers are proficient at all three phases of the takedown.

To become good at taking down your opponent, you must first be able to think from a defensive as well as an offensive standpoint. Besides being skillful, you must be strong from the tips of your fingers to the tips of your elbows. Keep your elbows close to your body and use your hands and forearms as a first line of defense to ward off your opponent's attempts to penetrate the area under your arms, where every wrestler is most vulnerable to a takedown.

STANCE

Assume a basic athletic stance. Linebackers, basketball players, golfers, and tennis players all use the same stance because it affords sudden movement with balance in any direction. Stand erect, feet approximately the same width as your shoulders. There are two common positions for the feet: the square stance and the lead-foot

Square stance

TAKEDOWNS

Lead-foot stance

(open) stance. In the square stance, the feet are approximately shoulder-width apart and parallel. In the lead-foot stance, sometimes referred to as the "sugar-foot stance," the feet are staggered. In both stances, the toes may point out slightly; each individual has his own preference, but we prefer to point the toes out to gain better balance.

Knees and hips are flexed to elevate or lower your body. Raising and lowering your body, referred to hereafter as changing levels, is a vital concept in wrestling. We will talk later on about changing body levels in different maneuvers.

Face your opponent and hold your head upright, always above your hips. Straighten your back at a slight angle from the waist. Your elbows are close to your side, hands in front, off your knees, palms down toward the mat. The tips of your fingers to your elbows are your battle weapons and should be ready for combat.

Your stance must enable you to move and penetrate your man's defense. To work your opponent into a desired position for a takedown, keep him constantly in motion until he reaches that position at which you think your attack will have the greatest chance of success.

Noncontact set-up

TAKEDOWNS

SET-UP

As you move, *set up* your opponent by making him react in some way that is advantageous to you or that will be later in the match. There are two kinds of set-ups: In **noncontact set-ups,** you divert your opponent's attention without touching him. Feint with your eyes, your feet, your hands and arms, with any part of your body. Reach for a leg and watch his reaction, or employ your hands like a boxer and jab at him as though you were setting him up for a big punch. You can also clap your hands or stomp your feet.

The second set-up is the **contact set-up,** in which you actually touch your opponent. Tap his head and upper body, or slap and drag his elbow or tie up his collar—all for the purpose of watching how he reacts. Use any one of these set-ups or any combination of them to help in your takedown attack.

Single leg

Contact set-up

Single leg

TAKEDOWNS

PENETRATION

Attacking from the correct stance, you *penetrate* your opponent's defense by driving toward and through him, aiming for an imaginary spot behind him, just as a boxer does when he hits through his opponent. Following through insures penetration. Why is penetration important?

Suppose you were asked to carry a 50-pound bag of sand. Would you stand at arm's distance and try to lift the bag, or would you move next to it and lift it using your arms, back, and legs? When your legs are stretched out, your arms fully extended, and you do not have full use of your back and legs, lifting a bag of sand or an opposing wrestler is a formidable task. To correctly pick up your opponent in wrestling, you must use your legs and back: Penetrate in close to his body, smack his thighs, drive through him, straighten, and lift him up off the mat.

To improve your penetration, use the **drop-step drill** and practice this every day in three stages. First, line up against one wall of the wrestling room. Using as a lead foot, for example, the left foot from a

Lead foot to drop step

Penetration from drop step

square stance, step and stretch as deep and as far as possible. This long step draws the right knee down toward the mat and the chest down near the left knee. From toe to toe the distance may be 6 feet. We describe this as 6-foot penetration. Next, move your right foot up behind your left heel and stomp the mat—a movement that signifies the correct abruptness and quickness—then push off on your right leg until you reach the stretching limit again. Bring up the trailing leg, keep your head and back straight over the left knee, and repeat. The first time you perform this drill, do 6 to 10 repetitions across the mat and the same number back. Step slowly at first but gradually speed up, until you can do them rapidly.

    The second part of the drill requires two men. Your partner stands 6 feet in front of you. Repeat the same penetration drill as before. As you move to your full extension, your chest should collide with your opponent's legs at the thighs. As you straighten your shoulders and back, lift up your opponent and, still on your knees, carry him 4 or 5 steps. You will appreciate the idea of driving through him and the virtue of elevating him because once he is in mid-air he has no balance and his power is neutralized.

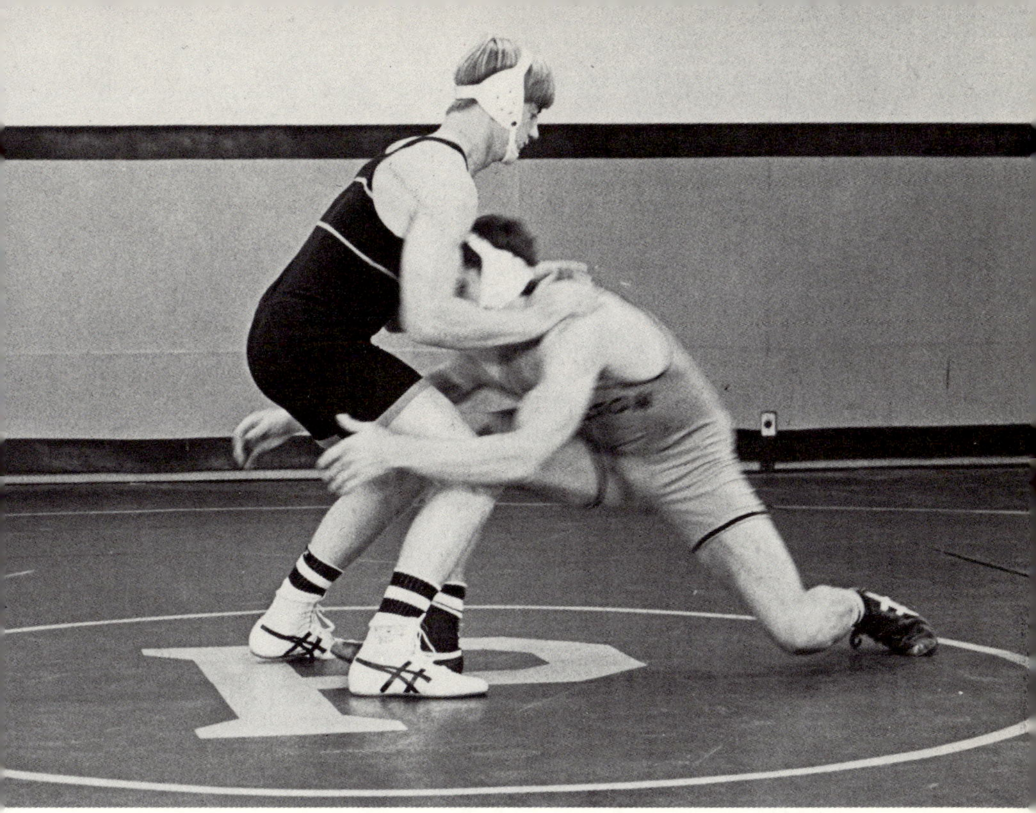

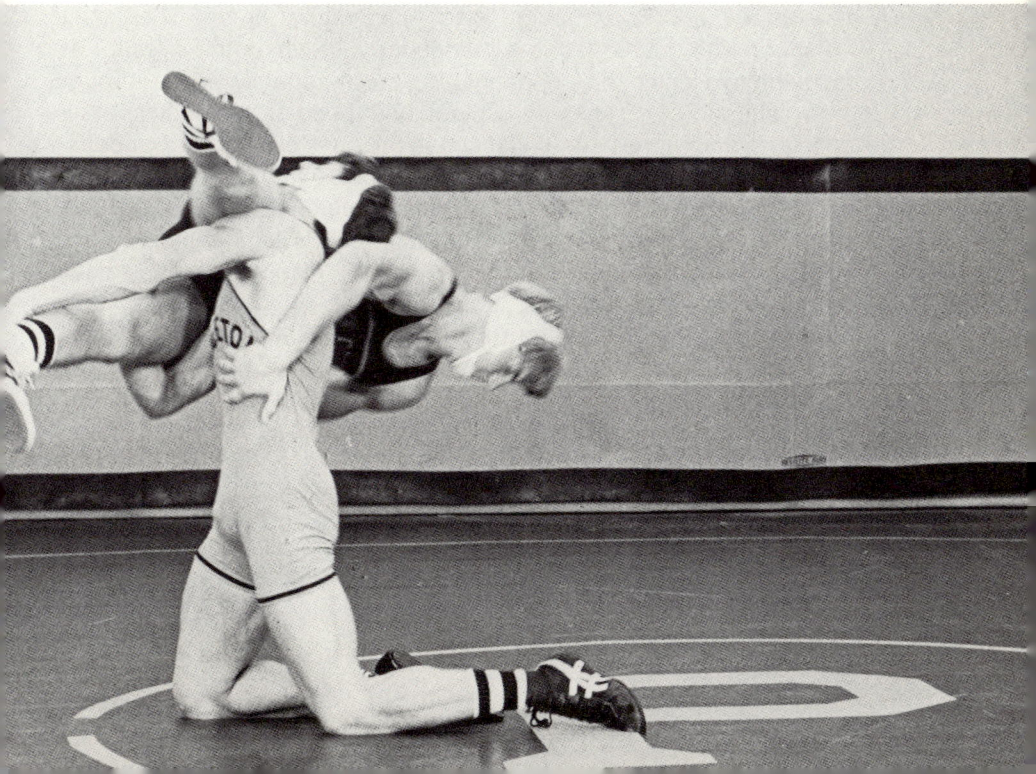

FINISH-OFF

To set your partner down in a proper *finish-off,* reach across and grab the heel on the opposite side of the arm you reach with. If you use your right arm, grab his right leg and pull it up toward your right shoulder to force him down on his hip. He has now lost the use of his legs for his defense. Repeat the routine 4 or 5 times across the mat, then switch partners.

A common mistake in penetration is for the attacking wrestler to lift his lead foot and place it down in almost the same spot he started. Take a bold step and drop to the knee. It is very important to lean over the lead foot. This extra penetration can be important to the success of your move.

The *drop-step penetration drill* is an excellent drill for developing an effective double-leg takedown.

Takedown maneuvers can be divided into several categories: those that aim at the upper body, those that combine lower and upper body targets, and those that attack the legs. A successful wrestler must also be able to initiate takedowns against a kneeling opponent.

LOWER BODY TAKEDOWN MANEUVERS

In attacking the lower body, the double-leg takedown is the most elementary and commonly used, especially among beginning wrestlers. The double leg is a maneuver with which the wrestler attacks the two legs of his opponent. As you, the attacker, drive through your man, aim at his knees and place your head on the outside of his legs. Lock your hands either just above the back of the knees or below the buttocks to immobilize his legs. This prevents him from throwing his legs backward and lowering his hips for defense. The force of your deep penetration and drive and the lock on his legs causes him to topple backwards. After you double-leg your man, lift him up, reach across, and grab his opposite leg, setting him down on his hip. As he falls, release your hands from around his legs and spread out your arms for balance so that he cannot roll you. Keep the heel of your tripping leg behind his heel to block it when you fall. Follow up immediately with a ride such as a lace, a deep waist, an inside crotch–far arm, or some other controlling position.

Another finish-off for the double leg is to go in deep and stand right up with your opponent. Do not go to your knees. This move requires

Drop step to double-leg lift

tremendous leg strength. Once you get him into the air, lift him up to shoulder height. With your right hand, go to the inside crotch. With your left hand, work a half nelson on the upper body. Slowly and carefully lower him to his back to finish off the takedown. Still another finish when lifting is to sweep out the man's legs, lifting them across to the opposite side, to force his hips to the mat.

In the drill for the **double leg,** we prefer the opposing wrestler to use a square stance to make it easier for the attacker to split or step between his legs. Proper drilling distance is determined by having two wrestlers stand with arms forward, fingers touching. This distance forces them to step hard for penetration.

Low single leg

Encasing single-leg foot

Remember: If you fall short on penetration, you will try to reach with your arms—think of the example of picking up a 50-pound sandbag without benefit of your back and legs. Get inside your man's arms on your drop step and lift him straight up in the air.

The **single leg** is the most common takedown used in college wrestling. Unlike the double-leg takedown, where the head is on the outside and the attack aims at the knees, in the single leg the head is on the inside and the attack aims as low as possible on the leg, preferably at the ankle.

Take a deep, penetrating step, but instead of splitting your opponent's feet, step to his side and drive your shoulder into his shin. Your outside arm on the same side as your lead leg (let's say the right arm) swings behind the heel of your opponent's leg as you take your drop step. Your near left arm grabs the heel. You now have that ankle and foot encased in your arms. The next move depends on position. If you drive head-on at your man and push straight into his shin with your right shoulder, the shoulder pressure on the side of the lead foot forces him to fall backward.

Single-leg finish-off

Another finish-off to the single leg, as you encase your man's foot in your hands, is to step with your trailing leg 180 degrees around and behind your opponent. Quickly lift up his foot and hold it tightly against your chest, taking it as high as you can. The higher the leg is lifted, the harder it is for your opponent to maintain balance. Be sure you hold his leg at the ankle. Do not let him use you to stabilize himself, but pull as you lift in order to knock out his only supporting point.

Still another finish-off for the single leg, once you are behind your man, is to place your lead arm in front of his far leg, trapping it at the ankle. As you start to press against the back of his leg with your shoulder, he begins to lose balance and to fall forward. Continue the forward pressure, then lift your shoulder and force him down. Remember that the lower you go on his legs, the greater chance you have for success. Conversely, the higher you are, the easier it is for him to counter.

Height is crucial with single leg

Cross pressure to destroy base

UPPER BODY TAKEDOWN MANEUVERS

The **duck under** is a finesse takedown in which the attacker ducks under his opponent's arm, uses his head as a lever, and drives his opponent to the mat. As in all takedowns, penetration is essential. In this case, you are not only trying to go through the man but behind him. There are three other keys to this maneuver. You must change your elevation in order to get under the arms of your opponent. To get under him, you must force him to extend his arms to create a gap for ducking through. And, you must shoot to his hip.

Let's look at a couple of set-ups for the duck under. From a neutral position, control your opponent with your right arm on his collar and your left hand either on his elbow or on the inside of his arm at the bend in his elbow. (Remember, tips of fingers to tips of elbows.) With your left hand, make a V-shape with your thumb and forefinger and shove that into the bend in his arm, trying to force his elbow behind his back. What is his reaction? He should offer resistance. Draw your elbow toward your body to encourage the extension of his arm. When his arm is extended, a gap will open under his armpit. Drop your chin to your chest as you change elevation by lowering your hips and knees. While you do this, thrust your head up under his armpit, behind his shoulder. You should face the same general direction as when you started the move, but your head is behind his near arm, your body is tight to his side, your other arm still controls his neck, and your free arm, the one that was pushing into his elbow, has now wrapped around his body. You can take him down in one of two ways: If you have had sufficient pressure on his collar and have started to bring his head down toward the mat, place your left arm behind his right knee and lift. Then spin him around on his single supporting leg, pulling his head downward and lifting his leg upward. This finish-off is more popular at the elementary level.

In advanced competition, once you get your head behind your opponent's shoulder, the best finish-off, is the *lift and jerk* or *trip*. Encircle his body with your left arm, then release his collar and lock your hands. Interlock on the same side you have just gone under. Immediately apply pressure downward with the right arm on his near leg, the one closest to you. From this point, you might lift him and drive his hips forward, releasing both your hands from his waist and moving them underneath his shoulder. Pull his shoulder back toward you as he falls.

Forcing arm extension in duck-under set-up

Duck under: penetrating with head under arm

Lift and jerk

Front pressure trip: With the hand locked around the body and the pressure down on the opponent's near leg to stabilize him, lower your level and pick up your man. Kick out his near leg so that when he starts to fall there will be no leg to support him. Once the leg is kicked out, force him down to his near hip—and stay alert for a switch or sit-out as he comes in contact with the mat.

When your opponent takes inside control of the tie-up with a collar and/or a bicep, you also have the possibility of a duck under. Place your arm over his collar-controlling arm and hook his elbow. This is described as an overhook of the elbow. When you do that, you im-

Elbow hook to set up duck

mobilize his arm although he still has a tie-up on your collar. But as you extend his arm, drop the level of your hips, slip your head under his arm and get behind him by stepping deep and coiling around him. Then, take him down by either one of the same two methods just described.

You can also perform a duck under from the underhook series. Underhook with your right arm under your opponent's armpit and lock onto his shoulder. With your free arm, grasp his wrist or bicep, or make feinting pushes against his far shoulder. As you control his near side with your right arm underhooked, extend his arm on his far side and take a deep step with your left foot tight to his body, lowering your elevation, head under his armpit, and—still with tight control—moving your head beyond his armpit. Then, straighten up and place your ear against the back of his shoulder so he cannot lift or swing his arm up over your head. Once under his arm, let go of the underhook and lock your arms around his body as you did previously.

Underhook to near-side duck

TAKEDOWNS

Another set-up from an underhook is to draw your opponent's near leg toward you. As he shifts his weight to that leg, lift his elbow to create a gap that your head can penetrate. Your head follows his shoulder from front to back. It is important to note that when you underhook an opponent your ear should lie on his shoulder and you should shove your forehead into his neck as you hold tightly with the underhook.

A **cross duck under** is a good response to double wrist control by your opponent. Pull on his left arm. When he resists, quickly pull on the right arm and duck under that side. On one side, you have feinted him and led him to believe you were going to that side; once he starts to react, you have to move to the other side fast.

Cross duck under: faking left

Cross duck under: completing on right

Arm drags: The arm drag is executed in its simplest form by holding your opponent's wrist and upper arm and going behind him while bringing him to the mat. There are three ways to set up the arm drag:

1. You grab your opponent's wrist, lead it across your chest with your free hand and hook his arm above the elbow. Go to him—do not pull or drag him to you—and trap his shoulder in your armpit. You have exposed his side; now, follow up by going behind him and locking your hands around his body. Trap his near arm to his body. You can finish off the takedown with a front trip or a lift.

2. When your man grabs your wrist, he feels he has good control and is not jeopardizing his position; this can give him a false sense of security. Lead with your wrist, which he is holding across your chest. At this point, he still has control of it. Move your hooked arm the same way as in 1. above, then bang your wrist on the side he controls. This will pry loose your wrist. As you do this, hook and go behind him.

Arm drag when opponent controls

Arm drag when opponent controls

3. Use the *circle drag*. Your hands face your man. Grab his elbow from the outside, letting him have an inside tie-up. Raise your palm as if waving to him, drop it to the outside and, as you bring it inside to tie up, karate-chop his control off your arm. Pass the arm across his chest and, with your free hand—your hooking, or dragging, hand—grasp his arm above the elbow and continue your drag. Circle him and lift up your palm, chopping down at his hand to free your elbow. You can work this from a full circle or from a half circle. If you have an inside tie-up, raise your palm and wave; as you do, cut to the outside, forcing his arm across your chest, then hook and cut behind. Remember, you want to go to the opponent rather than drag him to you. Make sure you have full control of the arm you have hooked under your armpit. The safest maneuver behind the man is to go right away to a lock, trapping one of his arms in the lock.

Circle drag

Circle drag

The **shrug:** This takedown is used as a finesse move when the defensive wrestler charges you. The defensive wrestler has a collar tie with his right arm. Overtie him with your left arm behind his neck. Both of you are now facing each other. Let him resist your overtie, and as he does, turn sideways. Look behind and shrug the shoulder nearer the controlling arm. This drives off his collar control. Wedge the shrugged arm behind the elbows toward the armpit, and just carry him through. His momentum will help you guide him forward; you then take a deep step, lock around his hips, and control and pressure his near leg.

Shrug

TAKEDOWNS

COMBINED UPPER-LOWER BODY TAKEDOWN MANEUVERS

The **cross elbow and knee snatch:** This technique aims at the knee and occurs out of a tight tie-up. Place your right arm on the collar, left arm on the elbow of your opponent. Squeeze the elbow in toward his chest while tightly holding his head. Release your right arm from his collar and carry his elbow across his chest, pushing it into his chest. As you do, step in with the near or right leg. This will bring his right knee in close to you. With your right arm, snatch his knee. Once you get it, release his elbow and clasp both hands to the knee. Put your shoulder into his thigh and, keeping your hands locked behind his knee, push against his hip joint. He is on one leg, and has no balance. Set him down on his right hip.

Cross elbow to knee snatch

The **head spear to knee snatch:** To use the head as a spear, take a bold step and point your head at his short rib. Bend at the knees to get low. If you have a right-foot lead, it is the right foot which takes the bold step, to his right side. As you spear the short ribs, snatch his knee, grabbing it outside with your hand, at the tendons. Do not go high or low on the knee. Motion is critical in this takedown. You must move your opponent backward so he has no balance. Secure his leg with elevation and down pressure. Then step to the front or side to turn him at least 180 degrees.

Head spear to knee snatch

Head spear finish-off

High-crotch takedown: Use with the same tie-up as a cross elbow and knee snatch. Right arm on your opponent's collar, left arm on his elbow. Lead with the left foot, put pressure on his elbow, and drive it across his chest. When he resists, lift his elbow and step deep, placing your lead foot behind him. Transfer your arm from his collar to his crotch, but do not reach around his leg. Go straight up the crotch toward the beltline. A common fault is to lock around the leg. At this point in the takedown, you have to decide how to finish off the move, a decision which depends partially upon your opponent's reaction. If you do not trap his near knee tightly with your left arm, pinning it to your chest, then you must continue around your opponent, stabilizing him with the high crotch and finish off as in a duck under. If you do trap the near leg, then you can finish off as in the double leg with a back

Elbow-pressure set-up to high crotch

Penetrating step in high crotch

Trapping near knee in high crotch

heel trip or by lifting and returning to the mat with a crotch and half nelson.

There is one other set-up in the high crotch to be used especially when the man ties up with you. Hook his elbow as you did in the duck under, but instead of ducking, lift on his elbow, reach for the high crotch, and go through the same process, applying pressure on the near knee.

Common mistakes in the high crotch are to not drive your opponent's arm across his chest and to not reach directly up the crotch.

TAKEDOWNS

37

High-crotch transfer to double leg

Underhook series: As a reference point, the right arm is the underhook arm; the left arm, the block arm. Two basic ways to get into the underhook are:

1. Block your opponent's far shoulder with your left hand. As soon as you do, your right hand shoots out midway between his armpit and hip, through the imaginary hole, up behind his shoulder. Your palm is now on top of his shoulder.

2. Shoot a weak single leg. Come up to your feet with your right arm in an underhook. Be careful: An underhook tie-up is risky if you linger in it because it sets up your opponent's high-crotch move. Your left arm, the block arm, must be ready if he is a good high-crotch man. Block his far shoulder so he cannot go under.

After you are in the underhook, push, pull, and swing to your man to get the feel of control. The underhook arm (also known as the kip-up arm) extends toward the sky to eliminate your opponent's defense on the underhook side and open him for attack. From the underhook set-up, bear-hug your man, dropping around his waist and locking your hands on the far side against the floating ribs. Immobilize his hips,

Underhook tie-up

TAKEDOWNS

Underhook tie-up to arm extension

WRESTLING

then move him forward or backward, depending on his position. If he leans forward, hip lock him to the mat. You have to change levels: Bend your knees and step in front of him so your hips are now under his center of gravity and you can lift by straightening your legs and throw him. Once you throw, post your hands on the mat to secure your balance. Remember to stay in a good high position over him.

Bear hug: hip immobilization

Bear hug to hip loc

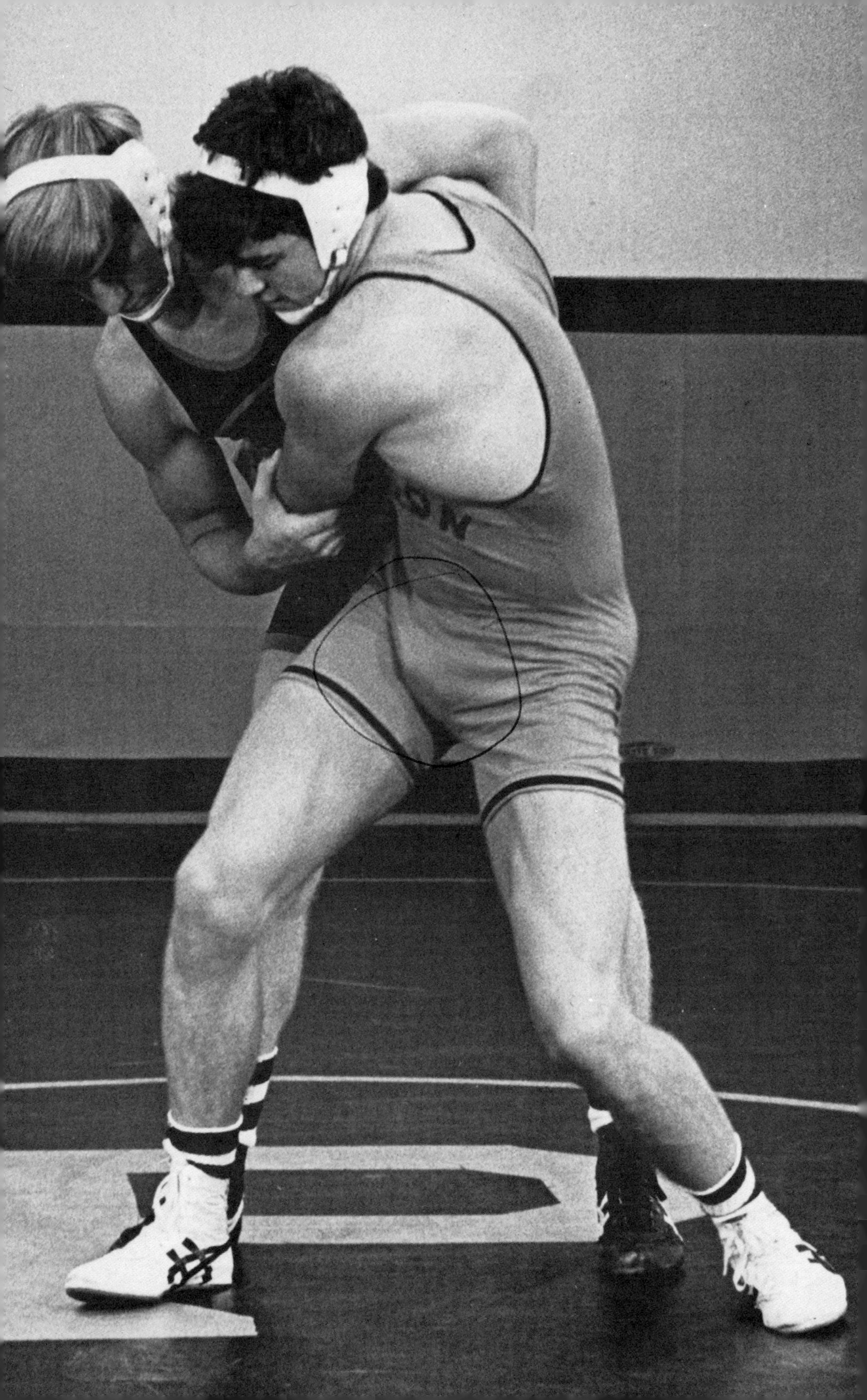

Another way to finish off—if he straightens up—is with the **bear hug.** Place your ear (in a right arm underhook, the right ear) to his sternum. Put your right knee behind his left knee and block forward at the knee joint, rotating him 180 degrees with the lock, moving your head in his chest as a level. Push him to his back, keeping your head on the chest to ensure height and an advantageous position.

Underhook to duck under: After you secure the underhook, your opponent will sometimes try to counter it by locking your wrist. When this happens, you can execute a duck under. You have the underhook and have his wrist with your free hand. Underhook with your right arm and grab his wrist with your left. With your left foot, step boldly straight into him; at the same time, raise your wrist to open a space between his arm and his side. Duck under, remember to change levels, go behind and lock.

You can use the same move if he ties up your wrist. Bring your tied-up hand away from his body to create a gap. Draw him toward you by stepping back with your left foot to force him forward. If he attacks, step forward yourself and duck under. The main point is to extend his arm away from his body so you can go underneath.

After you establish the underhook, you are ready to execute a three-phase offense, *straight pulls* to *swings.*

Straight pulls: From a right-arm underhook, pull the man toward you and step back. He will react. Suppose he responds by leading with his inside leg, the one closest to the underhook side—let's say the left leg versus a right underhook arm. Your straight pull exposes one leg for a single leg attack by you. Withdraw the underhook arm, drop step, and attack below his knee. If you cannot get below his knee, go for the high crotch, but do not go to the mat. Attack high in the crotch, the higher the better. The closer you are to his body, the easier to get your center of gravity under him and pick him up.

If, when you pull him toward you, his feet assume a parallel relationship (the square stance), attack him with a double leg and split his feet, a second takedown off a straight pull.

A third takedown off a straight pull is the **heel pick.** Your opponent reacts to your straight pull by stepping toward you with his far leg, exposing his far ankle. Drop step to his far ankle (change your lead foot), bringing your underhook arm down across his support foot to stabilize his base. You do not try to pick up his heel as much as you try to stabilize his heel and scissors his upper body.

A **swing set** is the most effective way to set up the underhook series. Your right arm underhook is the reference point. Step deep into

Underhook: straight pull to single leg

your man with your right foot and turn 180 degrees, dropping the left foot behind him to make him swing his outside foot. As he steps, he transfers his weight to that foot and sets himself up for a heel pick on his far ankle.

If he does not swing but lands with a square stance, attack him with a double leg. If he does not swing at all, his inside leg should be exposed for a single-leg attack.

Underhook set to double leg

Underhook swing set to heel pick

Underhook swing set to heel pick

TAKEDOWNS

If you pick his heel and he is able to withdraw that heel, he is now set up for a **pancake.** Pull down on the overhook arm and shoot your underhook arm up to his opposite side. Both of you now face each other on your knees. Slap his knee with your overtie hand, the hand on the same side he has underhooked. He drops his knee back, weakening his base. Pull down on his underhook arm, and up with the underhook and pancake. Finish off with a pull and heel pick.

The **barrel roll** is a takedown that requires a combination of legs and arms. A good set-up for the barrel roll is the collar-bicep tie-up. With your left arm on your opponent's bicep and right arm on his collar, step back slightly to force him to shift his weight—this is one of the keys to the barrel roll. Lock your left arm behind his elbow—another important step—then pass your head under his armpit. You have his arm locked around your head with your left arm and have stabilized his right leg. Drop to your outside knee (left) and split his legs with your right knee. At the same time, reach up his crotch with your free (right) arm, another essential step. Hoist him off the mat an inch or two to remove any base. Keeping your left knee down, sit toward your left hip. Bend your chest toward that left knee and carry him over your shoulders. You must move your chest to meet the knee. It is a common error for the attacker to fall over backward because he

Barrel roll

does not bring his chest to meet the down knee. At no time do you relinquish control of his arm. Your head was under his armpit, but you now slide it out so that it blocks his chest. This makes it difficult for him to get back to his knees. Turn him toward his back and continue to pull tightly on his arm as you meet him chest to chest. (You should get 2 points for control and also 2 or 3 points for the near fall.)

Once you meet him chest-to-chest, finish off with a reverse or half nelson and body press.

We refer to another version of the barrel roll as a *fireman's carry*. You are in the collar-bicep tie-up and he has overcommitted. Grab his right elbow and drop your head under his armpit, as in the barrel roll. Hold tight on the arm, and fall to both knees at an angle perpendicular to him. Reach for the crotch, and this time go around the leg. Instead of going to the roll, hoist him up as if he were a board across your shoulders and throw him over your head onto the mat. Once you throw him he will usually land on his side; you then have to drop immediately down on him; you will meet him chest to chest and should hold him on his back for near-fall points.

Fireman's carry

TAKEDOWNS

Fireman's carry

The **dump,** another member of the barrel roll family, is primarily a counter to the single leg and is best used when the opponent reacts to your single leg attack by sprawling and undershooting your free arm. With his hand under your armpit, trap his underhooked arm. Force the hooked arm down and lift behind the near knee in a manner similar to the barrel roll. The finish-off is exactly the same as in the barrel roll.

The **Russian tie-up** or **two-on-one:** From an open stance, grab your opponent's right wrist with your right hand; pass it across your chest. Hook his arm above the elbow with your left hand. Move toward him and stick your head between his shoulder and his head.

Another way to get into a Russian is to shrug his collar tie-up with your shoulder. Pinch your opponent's collar-tie arm with your opposite arm, hard against your chest. As you pop your shoulder and clear your collar tie-up, underhook the Russian tie-up arm with your free hand.

To transfer from a double underhook to a Russian, cover the lower arm with the hook arm above the elbow, trapping it, then releasing it with the wrist hand and coming over it. Now you are into the same Russian tie-up.

The Russian tie-up is an especially good defense for a wrestler who tries to protect his lead. If you control one of your opponent's arms, he cannot take you down.

The Russian tie-up leads into several moves, including the **crunch.** Secure a Russian. Maneuver yourself hip to hip with your opponent. Holding his wrist palm up, keep his arm straight and drive your inside shoulder into the back of his shoulder, still holding his wrist. Drop to the mat as he goes down, transfer the hook arm to the rear crotch, pull yourself up and over the man, and gain 2 points for a takedown.

Dump set: tight arm control

Block chest with head

Cover: chest to chest

Open stance to Russian tie-up
Shrug collar tie-up to Russian arm control

Shrug collar tie-up to Russian arm control

Crunch: arm pressure

From the Russian tie-up, you can drag an opponent who goes for cross wrist control. Let go of the hook arm, take the cross wrist and turn it into an arm drag on the far side, hooking his arm just above the elbow. Or go with a straight arm drag by releasing the wrist control and hooking above your outside hook arm (above the elbow), then short drag.

From a Russian tie-up, you can duck under: If he grabs your wrist control, use that wrist control, release the Russian tie wrist control, and duck to the far side. Extend his arm to make a hole to duck under.

From a Russian tie-up you can also go into a three-phase offense with straight pulls and swings, which we described in the underhook series, straight pulls. If your opponent shows an inside leg, shoot the single leg. If he shows a square stance, attack with a double leg. If he withdraws his opposite foot, then try the heel pick.

The next phase of the Russian tie-up is to swing your opponent. Take the Russian tie-up to his right arm (underhook arm is the left arm). Step back with the outside (right) foot. Pivot on your inside foot and drive him forward with your shoulder. As he steps boldly forward, change levels and pick the heel on his stepping foot. If he withdraws his foot, leaving the inside foot, attack with a single leg. If you get a square stance, attack with a double leg.

Drag from Russian tie-up

Duck under from Russian tie-up

Wrist control in Russian tie-up

Cross pressure to double leg

Swing set-up to heel pick

Swing set-up to heel pick

The next move from a Russian tie-up is a barrel roll. If you have his right arm in a Russian, step across with your right foot. That opens a hole under the underhook arm. Plant and drive back into him. Change levels and go under his arm. Trap his underhooked arm on your shoulder and, as you do, take your free (right) hand and either trap his leg or go up the crotch and take the barrel roll or dump.

Russian tie-up to barrel roll

TAKEDOWNS

Snap down

Snap down: The snap down is used mainly as a counter, a quick-hitting takedown. The offensive wrestler attacks your leg. Place one arm (right) on his collar, the other behind his elbow or shoulder. As he attacks, sprawl and cuff him behind his collar and arm, trying to force him to overextend his base. Your chest should hit his near shoulder and drive his head into the mat. Move the arm that was behind his armpit or on the elbow to his rear crotch and spin around him. Your hand on his neck must guide his head to the outside. A common mistake for a wrestler trying a snapdown is to guide the man right toward his legs instead of driving the head to the outside. Such an error allows him to follow through and regain his base, perhaps even achieve a takedown.

Throw-by: Another counter. This is an offensive move that results when the defensive wrestler tries for a double leg. Your first reaction as the offensive wrestler is to try to sprawl and break the lock of his hands. If you succeed, he should be on all fours. Grab his arm (right) and pull it across his chest so that he now has a three-point base—two knees and one arm. Your weight is on his back, not on his knees. If he pressures you, block his shoulder with your left arm and move him clockwise in a circle, picking up speed and momentum as you control him. He is now trying to save his position and is no longer on the attack. Once he has lost his sense of security and is merely trying to hang on, throw him by lifting and helping him to accelerate in that clockwise direction until he is overextended. His upper body whirls faster than his knees. Brake sharply and he will fall to the mat. You will fall, too, but on top of him. This is a skillful move and requires little energy.

Throw-by: control and motion

Throw-by: lift and extension

TAKEDOWNS FROM KNEELING-FACING

Many times both wrestlers find themselves on their knees still in a neutral position facing each other. This is referred to as *kneeling-facing*. Many takedowns can also be employed from this position. We have talked about arm drag, shrug, duck under, snap down, and throw-by, all of which, can also be worked from the knees in the same ways they would be worked if both wrestlers were on their feet.

2

Offensive Moves from the Bottom

Offensive moves from the bottom require less finesse but more explosiveness and strength. In order to be a consistently winning wrestler, you must know how to take your man down and you must be able to escape from the bottom quickly. Once the finesse part of an escape or reversal ends, you must scrap and battle and persevere to get out, all in a period of time shorter than when on your feet. You start your technique quickly, then follow up with explosive "gut" wrestling. Remember, too, that your opponent will apply his weight to you when you are on the bottom, something he cannot do in the standing positions.

Hand control is very important for escaping and reversing. If you can control one of the top wrestler's hands, it will be most difficult for him to maintain control or counter your offense. By the same token, never let your arms or hands get above your head, between your legs, or behind your back when you are on the bottom.

BASE POSITIONS

All offensive moves from the bottom are begun from two base positions: a four-point base known as the **referee's position** and a three-point base formed by both feet and the buttocks. In assuming the referee's position, keep in mind the image of a table top and its relation to its base or legs. A table with a large top and a narrow base is wobbly and unstable. The same is true for a wrestler on his hands

OFFENSIVE MOVES FROM THE BOTTOM

Referee's position

and knees in the referee's position. He must have a good base. Solidify your base by spreading out your knees and hands. Hands should be no closer than 12 inches to your knees, shoulder-width apart. They can be wider than 12 inches if necessary. You try to maintain that base while your opponent tries to break down that base.

The bottom wrestler wants to stay compact, head above hips, chest above thigh. In this crouch, you have a lower center of gravity and that is a factor in maintaining a good base. Your compactness also makes you more explosive. Too many wrestlers let themselves get overextended. They lose the explosive power needed to reverse or escape or even generate an effective offense. As the bottom man, you must work to get a good base, then work from that base to escape or reverse.

ESCAPES

Inside leg stand-up: At the whistle, initiate motion with your hands and head, thrusting your back into your opponent. Do not wait for him to move first. Your inside leg, the one closer to him, steps forward and plants on the mat under your chest. Bring up your other leg quickly. Block and cover—your outside hand covers his arm around your waist. Block off his other hand with your elbow. Clear the waist hand, controlling the fingers; with the blocked hand, push his wrist hand off your waist. It is not as important to

Inside leg stand-up: hand control

OFFENSIVE MOVES FROM THE BOTTOM

Inside leg stand-up: thrusting your back

Inside leg stand-up: clearing your hip

pull the hand away from your body as it is to clear it off your outside hip. Next, step forward on the same side that you cleared, cut back through, turning away from the hand you cleared. If you turn into the hand, he will tighten you up again. If you turn away, you unwrap his control. You have stepped out with the leg on the same side; now step back through with your trailing leg and square off, facing him with your hands out in front.

After you get to your feet, if your hands have not done their job, your man will lock his hands around your waist, making it hard for you to escape. You can counter this by raising his lock as high on your chest as

Stepping back for wing roll

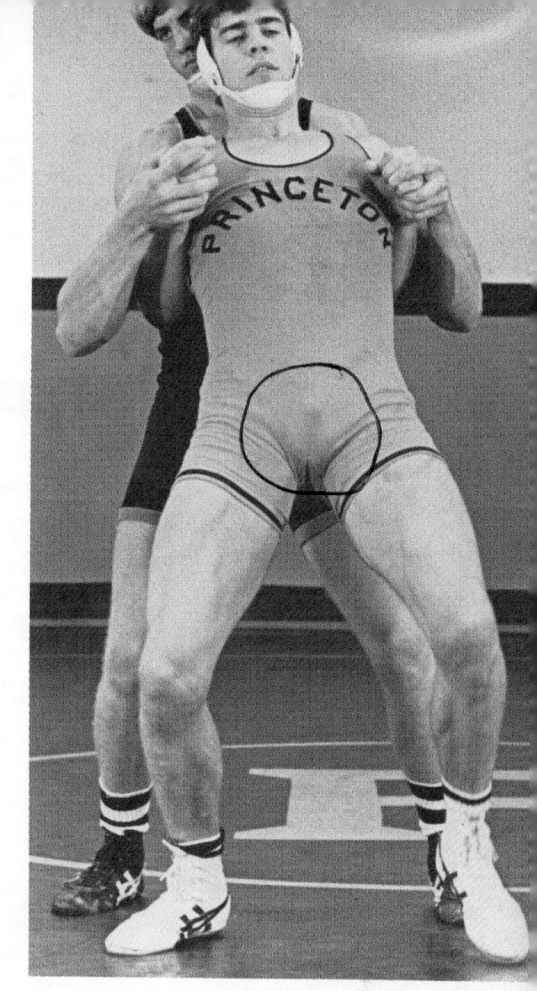

Raising locked hands high

you can. This upward motion frees your hips—you can step back and execute a wing roll, controlling his wrist and rolling him to his back. One method to break this lock is to bring the lock up to your chest and thrust both elbows down, breaking the lock, then blocking and covering his attack

Outside leg stand-up: In this less frequently used but still effective maneuver, push your head and back into your man. Step up first with your outside leg. Block and cover his hands. If you cannot isolate one hand, he will control you. Now do the same follow through, clearing your hip, stepping out, and spinning. An important point is that all stand-ups must be executed without hesitation and with tremendous force. If not, your opponent will probably set you back down to the mat.

Long sit-out: Used with the wing roll or switch, this maneuver can be very effective. By itself, it is not as successful. Start from a referee's position. Step up slightly outside with your outside foot to create a hole. Kick your trailing leg through that hole. Turn hard and face your opponent. Try to turn 180 degrees because the more you turn, the more successful you will be.

Short sit

Short sit series: Especially good from a three-point base. The main objective is to get to a sitting position as fast as you can. Many wrestlers throw their feet out in front. Others raise their outside legs. **Sit and post:** From a three-point, your hands must work, too. Block and cover, the same as in the stand-up. Clear the waist and place that hand on the mat, pulling it

OFFENSIVE MOVES FROM THE BOTTOM

Short sit: posting hand

to the mat by extending the elbow and using the weight of your body and your hand control to pin it. Now your opponent has only one arm for control.

Hip heist: When your man gives you a little pressure forward, push your head against his shoulder and, using his body as a support, raise your hips and hip-heist through.

Sit and push back: If your man normally pressures you from the top, push back from a short sit. Block and cover and, once on your feet, with your knees and hips flexed, clear your hip, step around, and face him.

Outside tripod: From a four-point base, at the whistle, block and cover, push back, and step up to an outside tripod using your inside knee and foot as the two inside supports and an outside foot as the third leg in the tripod. From this position, you can do several things:

1. Pivot on the inside knee, circling forward into your opponent; if he does not react, simply back out the back door, or back under the arm around your waist.

2. If he follows, which is most often the case, then wing roll, and as he begins his follow through, move your outside knee next to the inside knee, collapse, land on your elbow and side roll.

3. If he hangs over you, attack his free leg and with your free hand get wrist control, then roll.

Outside tripod

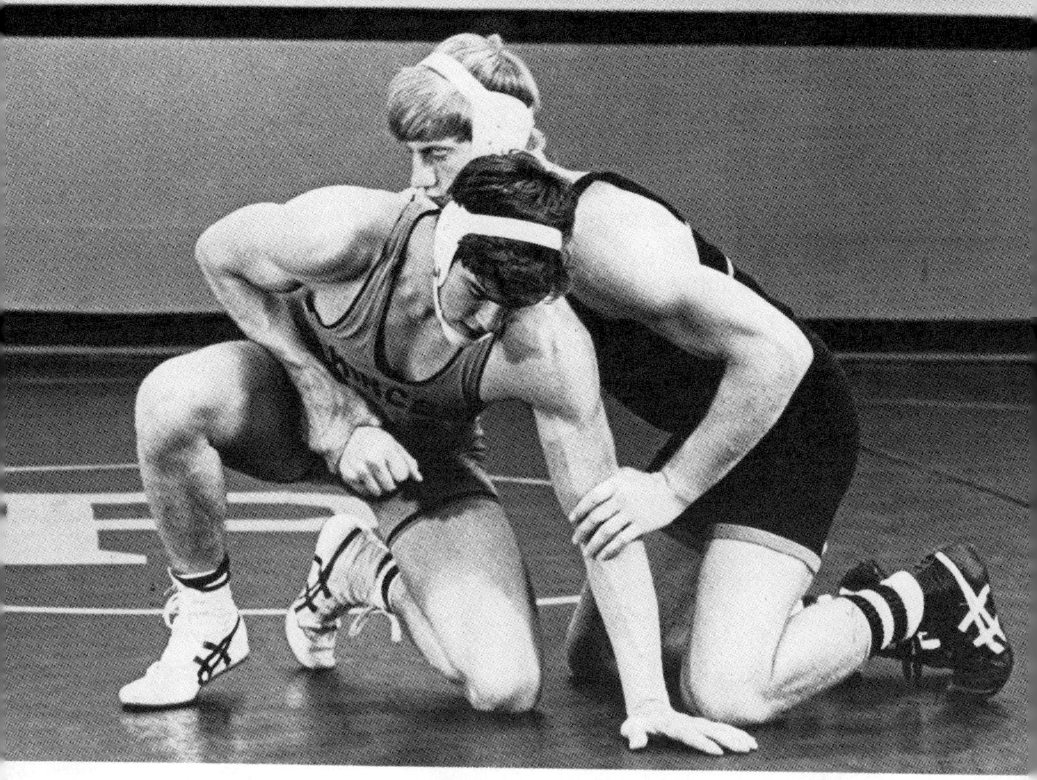

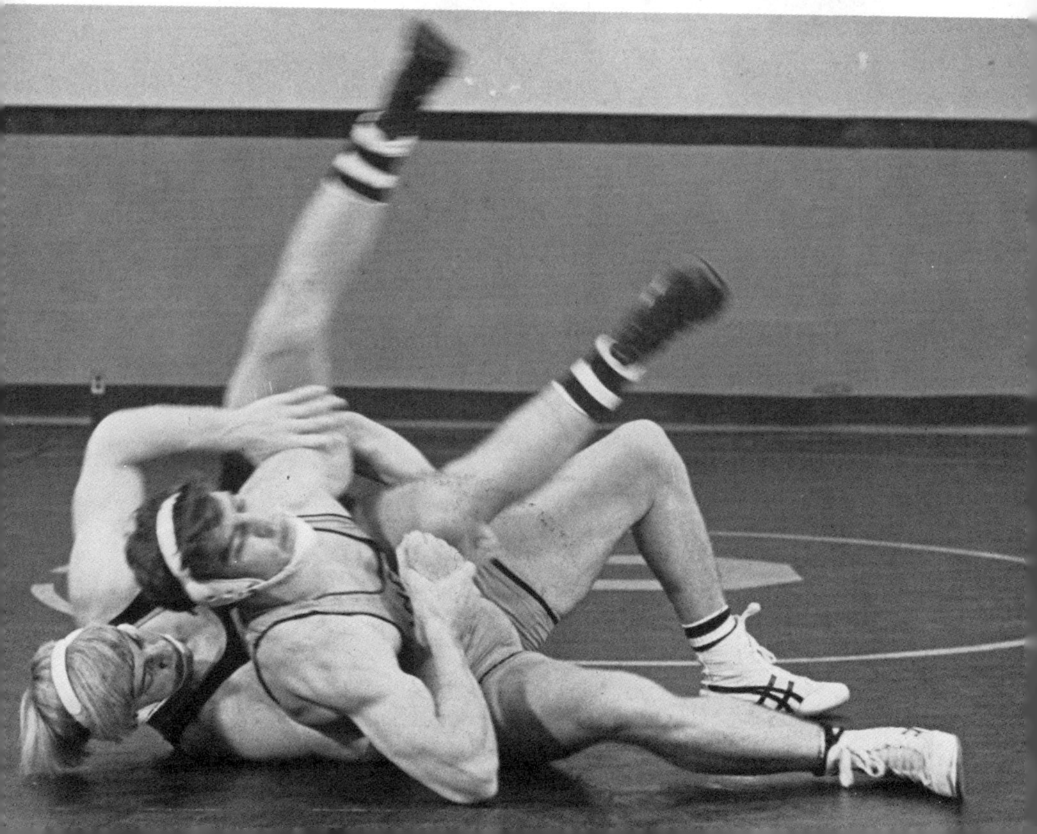

Scoot away: This maneuver is effective as a counter to an ankle and waist tie-up by the top man. You can escape if you will concede his ankle control temporarily. Clear out your waist first. After your waist is clear, step up with your inside leg, propel yourself forward like a sprinter off the blocks. Execute the same move again, a double leap, and turn toward your opponent. Never turn toward him on the first leap because a savvy opponent will follow you and hit you on your turn. With a double leap it is much more difficult for him to follow. Do not forget: After all escapes you should look for a takedown. The best time to shoot is just after a scoring maneuver.

Scoot away set-up: clear hip control

OFFENSIVE MOVES FROM THE BOTTOM 73

Scoot away: propelling forward

Hip-heist switch: Ten different coaches will give you ten different but effective switches. We believe the hip-heist switch is the best. Assume a good referee's position. As the down wrestler, you must sit over the inside leg, the leg on the side on which the top wrestler is aligned. Both feet are now in front of you as you sit back at a slight angle, not necessarily a right angle, but one about 30 to 60 degrees, depending on the power of your opponent and the techniques he likes. At this angle, lean your far side back into your opponent. As you move back into him, protect your hips from his control. Your outside arm goes over the arm locked around your waist to your opponent's inside thigh to gain leverage. Now you will find out the top man's reaction. Is he going to try to draw in your hips, or will he let you move and hope to come up with a reswitch? Let's assume you get the switch. Once you have an arm in his thigh and apply leverage, post your inside leg. Hip-heist, bringing your outside leg underneath the posted leg. This rotates your hips into a position of freedom, clearing the waist-controlled arm.

If he starts to pull your hips toward himself and to drive against your back, post your inside leg, quickly hip-heist, but this time, instead of pulling behind, windmill your leverage arm over his head and face off.

Hip-heist switch: heisting hips

Hip-heist switch: 180-degree rotation

Hip-heist switch: face off

Overhooks: Stand up with your outside foot. Bring your inside arm across your chest to free the inside elbow with the outside knee up. Next, transfer knees as you rotate the hips to move your outside knee down and your inside knee up, and rotate your upper body back toward your opponent. Drive your elbow shoulder height over his back. From here, drop your arm and hook his arm that is around your waist. Bring your fist to your chest and lock as tightly as you can on his arm above the elbow. Do another knee transfer, dropping your inside knee and posting your outside knee. Dump him flat with your hips by driving into him with sporadic bumps, not with static pressure. Once your opponent is flat, sit out to the front, prying on his crotch until you come out free to the front. If he steps over your leg to counter your overhook, then bump him to his far side and now and then smash your hips against his to wreck his base. Once he is flat on his side, post your arm behind his back, and swing your free leg behind your back. Sit on your buttocks on his far side and drive your chest forward over his chest. Scoop a leg, underhook a head, and finish off with a cradle or a half nelson and crotch. Sometimes the leg is trapped in this position, but don't be concerned as long as you can scoop up and get your cradle.

We have discussed the overhook as an offensive maneuver that complements an escape. A common counter to the overhook is to step over and bulldog the leg, then use a high leg over to escape from the bulldog counter.

Overhook: outside foot up

Overhook: rotating hips

Overhook: moving out to front

Sit-out and head check: In a shallow sit-out (or sit-back), you move your buttocks to almost right where your inside foot was posted in the referee's position. From the three-point base, as you sit and control the wrist of the arm around your waist, push back into him. Invariably, his head comes over one of your shoulders. If it comes over the outside shoulder (same side as hand control), then release your hand control, grab his head on top and pull it down between your hand and shoulder tightly, so he cannot turn it to either side. At this point, you have two choices: (a) you can turn to the free arm side, continuing to control tightly the head and come up with a half nelson at the end; or (b) you can drop to the controlled arm side, bringing your opponent along, and as you hit your side, hip-heist and turn free. If he does not drop his head over either shoulder, then push back into him, until your back straightens out almost parallel to the mat. This will break off his tight waist control and you can turn quickly inside and square off for a 1-point escape, similar to a long sit-out.

Sit-out and head check

OFFENSIVE MOVES FROM THE BOTTOM

REVERSALS

To reverse an offensive wrestler means to come off the bottom, where you were on defense, to the top, where you have control over the opponent.

The roll series is one of the best ways to reverse an opponent. The series consists of the *shoulder roll,* the *wing roll,* and the *bridge roll.*

Shoulder roll: This is usually performed from a sitting base although it can come from three different positions: (a) referee's position; (b) a sitting base; (c) a standing position.

In the referee's position you must remember that the top wrestler is trying to control two basepoints, your near arm and your hips or an ankle. In high school, the top man will go usually for the near arm and an ankle; in college, for the near arm and waist.

Shoulder roll from referee's position

Shoulder roll: moving your knee over your head

To generate offense, the bottom man must avoid having his near arm controlled. Keep it close to your body or side to minimize the loss of control. Keep your head up and stay compact. Reach between your far arm and far knee as though you were reaching for a dollar bill hanging from the ceiling. This forces your inside shoulder to the mat. Tuck your chin to your chest. In this upside-down position, move your knees over your head; this, then, carries your hips over your shoulders, creating momentum. Avoid the common error of falling toward your back. As you continue down in the roll, take control of your opponent's tight waist arm. This will tighten up and twist the arm in a rather unnatural but not illegal manner. As you come to your knees, finish off by coming through with a one-on-one and cover him with a near crotch or far ankle. Avoid going around his waist, for that would provide him with an immediate opportunity to respond.

Situation roll: Sit over your inside leg in a sitting base. Extend your near arm so that the palm of your hand is exactly next to your buttocks. Control your opponent's arm around your waist with your outside hand holding his wrist at the hand and wrist joint. Stay compact. To force your opponent to commit himself, jack up your hips and push back into him. He will invariably try to chop your near arm. As he

Situation roll: jacking hips with inside leg

Situation roll: continuation of roll

does, drop to your near shoulder, tuck your chin to your chest, and jack up your hips with the inside leg. Your toes should be curled in order to elevate your hips. Throughout you have retained wrist control of the tight waist arm. Finish off as you did in the conventional shoulder roll.

Standing shoulder roll: The higher above the mat your hips and chest are, the more difficult it is for the top wrestler to control you. The standing shoulder roll is set up by making your opponent commit himself from the referee's position. Give him a crack with your near hip as you come to a raised four-point base, knees off the deck, hips quite high, about equal to or above the head. A common error is that many wrestlers do not step the inside leg across and in front of the outside leg, which blocks the down wrestler in the middle of his roll.

As you make this critical step, drop to the top of the near shoulder. Your chin is now tucked to your chest. As you fall to your shoulder, push off with your inside foot, elevating your hips over your shoulders. As you start through the maneuver, roll across your shoulders, trap his waist arm, and finish off the same as in the other rolls of this series.

Perform the **wing roll** in a similar starting position from the bottom. Lean into the top man, pushing his far hand off your near elbow. As you knock off his hand, that reduces his control to the tight waist. His reaction is to drive back into you. As he does, control the tight waist arm, dropping to your far side, and post on that elbow.

A common error is to drop to the far shoulder. Instead, post the elbow. This forms an incline. As you drop to the far elbow, place your near instep against his thigh. This works him parallel and simplifies the job extending him. As you do, follow through by elevating him over your base. As he falls on his side, keep control of the tight waist arm. Work perpendicular, pressing your back to his chest. You can finish off in two ways: (a) stay in the perpendicular position and look for his near leg or (b) hip-heist through keeping the tight waist arm. This pressure vises his upper body between you and the mat. Then apply a nelson (half or reverse) coupled with an inside crotch and body press.

Bridge roll: To perfect a bridge roll, move into a tripod stance, forehead on the mat, both feet on the mat, buttocks up in the air. You can legitimately, but temporarily, break our rule about height and relation of head to hips. Let's say you have gone to a short sit-out. The top man chops you to your near side. That sets up the situation shoulder roll. If the shoulder roll won't go, drive your forehead into the mat and walk your hips up into the air. Depending upon how the top wrestler reacts, determine your course of action. Your first option is to

Standing shoulder roll: clearing near leg

Standing shoulder roll: height makes a powerful roll motion

Wing roll: forcing desired pressure

Wing roll: reacting to force

OFFENSIVE MOVES.FROM THE BOTTOM　　　　　　　　　　　　　　85

continue to pivot toward your opponent for a turn in reverse. Sometimes your opponent will follow you. Usually, however, the top man will release you and let you go free for the escape if he does not feel secure. But should he follow and crowd your hips, react with a wing roll. You have the wrist control. Now, catch his near knee with your near arm. Drop on your side to your hips, posting your far elbow; then elevate him. Lift and carry him across your body. He will land on his side and you can finish off as described in the side roll.

Bridge roll set-up: tripod position

Shoulder roll from near-side coverage

Trapping opponent's near leg

OFFENSIVE MOVES FROM THE BOTTOM 87

If the top man follows, but not tight to your hips, put your near arm in his crotch, right between his legs around to the outside thigh. Then, hip-heist through and elevate.

If the top man tries for a two-on-one or a one-on-one and he comes high, you can still grab his near knee and roll.

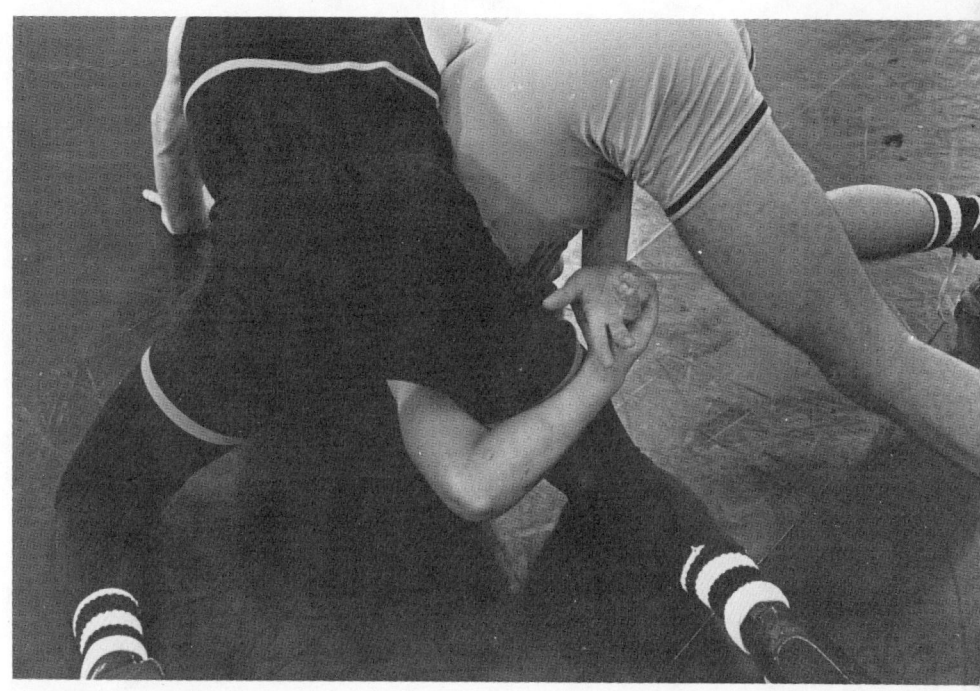

Near-arm and leg control

Throw back near leg to elevate upper body

Roll completion: posting on down elbow
Tight-wrist control: forcing into opponent

Pulling down on controlled arm; windmilling up arm

In yet another possible situation, you are on your forehead, you have wrist and near-knee control, but the top man lies back and presses against your upper body. You then work both knees up under your buttocks. Throw back your near leg to help elevate your upper body and knock out the inside torque of the top wrestler. Post on the down elbow—this gives you height with your upper body and forces the top man to slide down your body to his side. You still have the inside leg, so as he slides transfer to near knee control, then go through the same finishing-off process as before when he followed your hips.

The top man will sometimes come over the shoulder of the bottom man and take control of his wrist. Jam back into him, get off on a slightly parallel position to his near side or the side on which he has his arm over your shoulder. This move creates a tough position for him since you now control his balance. Keep turning into him and, as you do, windmill by raising your shoulder in the air. Pull down with the other arm. He cannot retain control and will lose balance, falling on his side.

3

Control and Pinning Combinations

CONTROL

You must know how to control your opponent after he has been brought to the mat. Successful riding depends on good balance, on controlling his leverage points—his head, legs and arms—and on taking the initiative. Previously we talked about the importance of the table principle for the bottom man. Your task as the controlling top wrestler is to deny the bottom opponent his table. Break his base, keep him broken down, control a hand and leg, and make him wrestle with some major disadvantage. The distribution of your body weight is also important. Make him carry your weight as much as possible so that he will tire faster. Keep your chest, your upper body weight, on the down wrestler's back. Remember: He will be constantly striving to create space between himself and you to improve his chance of escaping.

Change position to keep him off balance and guessing. If you have a good hold and he cannot move, do not release the hold, but try to improve it. The idea of constantly improving your position should always be a goal.

When you do change holds, transfer from one area to another, one at a time. Never transfer two areas at the same time.

Here are some other points to remember:

Always move with authority at the whistle. Never, never let the bottom man move first.

Avoid using the same first reaction each time at the whistle. Your opponent will likely catch on and adjust.

Analyze your position and know your relationship to the rest of the mat. If you are in control, right on the edge of the mat, turn your man so the direction of action is back toward the center. If you are working on his shoulders for a pin, direct the action into the center of the mat. Don't waste energy driving the down wrestler off the mat.

Never work from an off-balance position.

Once your opponent is prone, concentrate your weight on his upper body.

Remember that the bottom man will try to get your body parallel to his to facilitate his escape, so maintain a right angle with him when you break him off his base.

Control the waist and lower extremities first. Beginning wrestlers tend to work too high. They should generally check an ankle or rear crotch. If you ever go over your opponent's shoulder with one arm, the other arm should control a rear crotch or ankle.

Do not waste energy by tightening up for the sake of tightening up. Know when to tighten your hold.

Do not lose poise and confidence. A common mistake by a young wrestler who has trouble controlling his opponent is to become flustered and ease up.

As soon as the whistle blows to begin mat wrestling, the top man should check the leverage points of his opponent. He might check an ankle and arm, or a waist and arm, or a waist and ankle, or a far arm and a far ankle or a far arm and a near ankle. A high school wrestler usually checks a waist in combination with an ankle. In college, the wrestler will first control the waist and some part of the upper body, for instance, a waist and near arm chop, a near arm chop and inside crotch pry. This idea of establishing points of control or checking from the outset of mat wrestling is essential.

RIDING MANEUVERS

When riding your opponent on the mat, you should try to wear him down, opening up chances for pinning combinations. Be prepared to ride him at any point in the match, but particularly in the second and third periods, when you both start from the referee's position: One wrestler, the bottom, or down, wrestler, is stationary on hands and knees, hands spread approximately as wide as his shoulders. Legs are

CONTROL AND PINNING COMBINATIONS

parallel. The top, or offensive, wrestler is on the right or left side, on one or two knees, head along the midline of the opponent's back, with one arm around the waist, the other on his opponent's near arm, palm on the elbow. Control is the key word in riding.

Tight waist ride: At the whistle, press your near leg against the near knee of the bottom man. Pull him forward by chopping his near arm and tightening your waist control. Continue to block his near knee with your knee. In effect, you have forced the elongation of his body, making it difficult for him to regain his base.

Tight waist: near-arm chop

Inside crotch pry and near-arm chop: Your right knee goes behind his buttocks. Place the arm that was around the waist in the crotch, against the thigh of his outside leg. With your left arm, pull at the near arm and drive him forward onto his left shoulder. Retain your grip on his left arm, encircle his waist with your right and drive into him with your right shoulder. Do not lose your balance while you are driving him.

Ankle checks: We have already said that at the whistle the top man checks the leverage points to reduce the bottom man's chances for escape and reversal. If you check an ankle, quickly remove your arm from his waist when the whistle blows and grab the far ankle. With your other arm, come to the waist on the near side. Yank his ankle to force his heel up against his buttocks and turn his foot across his buttocks, inward, not outward. It is illegal to drive a limb or appendage unnaturally against its joint, so the foot must turn inward. As you drive on the ankle, you destroy one of the supports. Now hook the near arm. With the ankle and near arm hooked, you have forced his head down to the mat destroying his base altogether.

Another effective ankle check aims at the near ankle. Line up on the bottom man's right side, with your left arm around his waist and your right arm on his elbow. At the whistle, move directly behind him and scoop up his near leg or ankle. Drive it up hard and make the heel hit the buttocks right away. Turn the instep with the ball of his foot inward and force his upper body to the mat.

Ankle check

CONTROL AND PINNING COMBINATIONS

Every wrestler learns how to escape or reverse from the referee's position. If you can learn to control or stop an opponent on his weaker side, you gain still another advantage. Sometimes an opponent's offense is sadly weak on one side. Determine which side that is early in the match by changing sides in the referee's position.

Bulldog ride: This maneuver is used to control the lower extremities and is secured by a tight waist and near-arm chop. In the referee's position, your near knee should hit your opponent in the buttocks. This will help you secure the near-arm chop and the tight waist. It is more important to break his head down than his hips in this ride. Lace or overhook the near leg at the ankle so that his foot and lower leg are hooked between your upper and lower leg. Now move lower on his body and drive your shoulder into his buttocks. At the same time, pull back on the leg hook, as if you were trying to separate his leg at the knee. One force acts against the upper leg from one direction, another presses against the lower leg from the opposite direction.

The bulldog ride is a low hanging ride. Because you cannot hang there for long, try next to reach for a far ankle, break the man off his base, and, from there, go in for a lace ride. Or, with your near arm, pull the far arm back and trap it in the crotch. Once you have trapped his far arm in the crotch, release the bulldog hook and angle toward the upper body, knocking the man off his base. With his far arm controlled you are ready for a half nelson and a body press as you continue to drive him from his side toward his back.

There is another option for a pin. You have the leg laced. Catch

Bulldog hook on near leg of down wrestler

Lace ride

either arm in the crotch again, but give priority to the far arm. Unhook the bulldog and drive the man again on his side, breaking his base. This time, look for a near side cradle.

One-on-one and rear crotch ride: This ride is especially effective for stopping an expert shoulder roller. It is one of the best rides in wrestling. We can refer to it as either a bar arm or a one-on-one and a rear crotch. A good way to get into the bar arm and crotch ride is from a lace ride (also known as the navy ride, a maneuver where you have a one-on-one on the opponent's near arm with your head stuck into his navel, your other arm over his near leg and under his far leg).

The one-on-one and rear crotch ride works this way: Break his upper body by driving it toward the mat and at the same time lifting the crotch. This forces the down wrestler to react in one of several anticipated ways. The top wrestler must be slightly off the perpendicular toward his head. It is essential to have your weight high on his body (chest of top wrestler on the upper shoulders of the down man). If he tries to straighten out his arm, press your outside knee on his elbow as you pull the one-on-one into his chest to immobilize his arm.

When you have the man on his side in a lace ride and he starts to elevate himself in order to get to a base, execute the bar arm, and rear

CONTROL AND PINNING COMBINATIONS

crotch ride. Or, go into the ride as you would a bulldog ride—tight waist, near-arm chop with the near knee reinforcing the buttocks dump.

After you have broken your man to the mat with a one-on-one or the near arm, move your chest up on the back of his shoulders. As you do this, remove your arm from his waist and place it in the seam of the buttocks, or the crotch of his uniform. The bone in your forearm should drive into his buttocks. Simultaneously, grip him in the crotch. Be careful not to let your weight slide down toward the hip so much that the down man can elevate his upper body in an attempt to counter the ride. Concentrate your full weight on the shoulders of the down wrestler and bury his head in the mat. His upper body has to be held against the mat. The next step is to move off your knees onto your toes. This increases the pressure on him and helps wear him down. When he feels the added weight, he will usually try to free the bar arm by straightening the controlled arm. As it moves, position your far knee in the back of his elbow and pull the hand back toward his chest to immobilize it. This maneuver will convince him not to try moving his arm again.

After his arm is contained, it is likely that one of these desired reactions will occur: (a) he falls to his near hip with his back in toward your chest; (b) he leans away toward his far hip and faces you; (c) he jacks his hips up to sit on his lower legs.

If he should fall on his near hip so that his back is toward you, go into the back hook and bar arm series. Catch your back hook, release the bottom arm, move around the head and go into a body press and half nelson. What happens if the opponent turns to his far hip? You have immobilized his near arm so he cannot free it. What he does is lean toward the far hip. Remove your hand from his crotch and catch him right behind the knee of the near leg. Lift that knee high, parallel to the mat. Now, simply step into the Turk ride.

If, on the other hand, he exercises (c), stack him and force him into a shoulder roll, helping him along on his roll. As you lift him and carry him across both shoulders, he will be perpendicular to the mat with his buttocks up in the air. Throw him so that he continues through over his shoulder. Be prepared to backhook with the arm that you carried him through with. Catch his chin and jolt him back into your chest. This forces his shoulders closer to the mat. Straighten him out and break the momentum of his move. Once you have back-hooked him, then stick your chest onto his shoulder to secure him. Transfer the back hook to a bar arm: That is, release the back hook by coming out over it,

Step to Turk from one-on-one and rear crotch ride

onto the front side of his arm and go to the bar. You may want to hold his chin to settle him more with the reverse nelson, but you can tighten up by releasing the chin and going in front of the head with a half nelson. You can lock hands and bounce a little. Remember, whenever you are bouncing in a pinning combination, maintain at least a right angle to your opponent and, better, be slightly off that right angle, toward the head or shoulder. Too many young wrestlers come off the right angle toward the hip instead of the shoulders and that mistake allows the bottom man to work himself parallel to his opponent and place him in a tenuous position.

Once you have secured control with a tight ride, analyze your position and look for a pinning combination. Remember: When you work toward a pin, it is a good rule to take just a bit more time and make certain of the security of your hold rather than hurry and not have good control.

There are several near arm series pinning combinations that come off the tight waist ride coupled with near-arm control.

Head lever: This is a pinning set-up that can lead to a half nelson. After your man is prone, grab his near arm at the wrist. Drive into his near armpit with your head. Then, take a deep step with your inside

CONTROL AND PINNING COMBINATIONS

leg, driving your knee toward his head and lift his arm, pulling outward on his wrist. Slip the arm behind your head. As you drive your near knee up to his forehead and slip the arm, release his wrist; now, with an upright head, you have enough height so that he cannot free that arm. You are sitting on your near hip. Square yourself off in a slight hip heist. This will turn you directly perpendicular to him and prevent him from freeing his arm behind your head. A common temptation is to want to throw a half nelson immediately. Instead, place your hand on the mat, slide it under your opponent's head and lift. Drive him to his back. Once he is within 45 degrees of being pinned, employ the half nelson by reaching around his neck and grabbing his chin. Pull his chin and twist it at the same time as you lift on the tip of the head. By doing this, you prevent the bottom man from bridging and from using his head for leverage off the bottom.

It is worth digressing briefly to mention a common fault among young wrestlers working for a pin. They tend to put too much of their weight on the bottom man's hips or stomach. Rather, they should concentrate their weight and force on the down wrestler's upper body, from the pectoral muscles to the shoulders. (In high school, they must shut off their man's movement for 2 seconds, in college for 1 second.) Apply maximum force and pressure to the shoulders to cut off any defensive moves. If the man has gained good height by bridging, you might transfer your bar arm to the inside crotch and lift on the crotch to raise him enough so he cannot twist with his leg or shift his hips in any way. In this manner, you stabilize his hips and upper body. If he continues to squirm, release the crotch, go to a bar, tighten up and perform the coup de grâce.

Once you have broken a man with a tight waist and near-arm chop, pin him or gain quick back points with a **reverse winglock.** With waist control and your opponent prone, hook the elbow of the near arm (up arm), the arm you chopped. Shift your weight to his upper back. Hold the elbow so it is against your side, the tip just above your back. If the elbow is in your stomach or too near his chest or side, then you cannot effectively complete a reverse winglock. If the arm is not in correct position, do not swing the arm around the head. Keep it locked in against your side. You are now in a tight armlock. Swing, stepping boldly around the head, changing your body temporarily from a perpendicular to a parallel angle with your opponent, returning to a right angle on the other side of him. As you swing the arm around the head, twist the bottom man and force him toward his back. With your free arm, execute a reverse nelson. With the nelsoned arm, grab his chin and pull it back tightly. One shoulder might still be a couple of

Reverse winglock: locking up on high arm

Reverse winglock: spinning around head

CONTROL AND PINNING COMBINATIONS

inches off the mat, his back slightly inclined. Pull on the arm and on his chin and settle him to within 1 inch or so of being pinned. Then release the chin and go around the front with a half nelson, applying the final pressure for the fall.

Another option in the near arm series is a **tight waist and near-arm control at the wrist.** From a referee's position, lock your opponent's near wrist to control the normal bending of the arm. Move the captured wrist forward along your opponent's side. As you do, usually his hips will start to come up, too. When you work up on the body, you unavoidably reduce the pressure on his lower body. That is nothing to worry about. Once an opponent is prone, forget the lower area and work from the waist up.

As he starts to crank up his hips, pressure his upper torso. Put your forearm across his tricep or back. That will pin his shoulder in that position. If he can jack up his hips, he can do a lot of things, but he cannot move that near shoulder or near arm. Release the tight waist. If you have his shoulder pinned solidly, then with the waist arm, grab behind his near knee and lift. This transfers all the weight of the down man onto his far knee. As you lift, the pressure comes off that near

Trapping opponent's arm with your forearm

shoulder. Drive across the base leg, directly perpendicular, into him, knocking him to the far side. With the leg lifted and still controlled you can step into what we call a **Turk ride.** You have an opportunity to go to a leg series now, but suppose you do not go into legs. You still have that bar arm tightly controlled. Release the knee and go to the inside crotch.

We should consider at this point the question of when to take an inside crotch versus an outside crotch.

Take an outside crotch against a man who is still in a sound base. When he is broken down to his side and you are driving him from the perpendicular to his back, then take the inside crotch once his back is at an angle of less than 90 degrees to the mat.

You have that bar arm, have let go of the knee, and can go to the inside crotch. With the one-on-one and inside crotch, you don't yet have a pinning situation, but you do have good control. To turn it into a pinning situation, stay with the crotch, release the one-on-one and go to the half nelson or the reverse nelson. A half nelson would be best here, a deep half—as deep as you can get it. Place your chest on the chest of the down man and drive.

Once you have stabilized the bottom extremities, release that inside crotch and go to a bar on his top arm where you left the one-on-one. He will try to work his top arm between your bodies if he is a good wrestler. Therefore, bar that arm. So we are back to the same finish-off we had with a general head lever—a half nelson and body press.

Another option in the near arm series occurs when you have your man's near shoulder pinned to the mat with your forearm. When he jacks up his hips, he tries to bring up his knees under his chest to regain a significant base. That usually makes it difficult to keep his near shoulder pinned to the mat. You lose a little control there, although you still dominate the situation. Reinforce the one-on-one on that near arm with your free arm. As you lift his arm above his back, put more pressure on his head and keep his shoulders temporarily on the mat around the waist again to create a bar, then with the original one-on-one arm, go into a half nelson. You have his down shoulders pinned to the mat. Drive him into a rolling, circular fashion with your chest against his chest. Force him onto his back with the half nelson, into the same situation you had in the previous moves.

CONTROL AND PINNING COMBINATIONS

Hammerlock: Let's return to the same near arm series where you have the man prone with a tight waist and a near arm. Trying to get a one-on-one, you lose control of the near arm but finally grab it and pull it down along his side, straightening it out. If he keeps his arm bent so that the palm is toward his chest, his arm perpendicular to his body, he can muster force. But if you pull that arm down near his side, he cannot pull it perpendicular because your pressure is greater than his strength. Once you get his arm extended, quickly grab a one-on-one and place his arm at right angles behind his back. This is commonly referred to as a *hammerlock*. It can only be taken at right angles in accordance with the rules.

Once you have the hammerlock, release the tight waist and work two hands on the hammerlock. Usually the bottom man will take his free arm and put it just under his shoulder in order to push back into you, thus relieving some of the pressure. That is a desired reaction. If he does not, force him to do so. Extend the hammerlock to a 100 to 120 degree angle and try to drive it across his back. When you do that, you force him to push back into you, a reaction you can use to your advantage.

When he pushes, stabilize that hammerlock across his back. Your chest is in the middle of his back at this point. Keep good upper body weight on him to momentarily stabilize his shoulders. Swing your free arm and pivot from a parallel position next to him to his controlled arm

Hammerlock

side on an angle of 90 degrees, still maintaining pressure with the hammerlock. Drive it across his back so that his far arm is still forcing him to push back into you. Now go beyond the 90 degree angle, up to 180 degrees. Keep the hammerlock and continue to drive in the same direction. With your free arm, weave up or hook underneath the free arm of the bottom man. As you weave and bar through the free arm, lock the wrist of that hammerlocked arm. Release your original controlling hammerlocked arm. Momentarily put it on his head as you continue around him. Once you have moved around to an angle of 270 degrees, scoop his head with the free arm just as you did in the head lever. Slide the hand under his head, lift, and drive him toward his back, meeting him chest to chest. Once you get him on the downswing toward his back, transfer to a half nelson, but always keep the hammerlock hooked. Back off slightly from the right angle toward the head trying to put on the final pressure and lock that will cause him to be pinned.

PINNING COMBINATIONS

Half nelson: After your opponent is broken down flat on the mat, drive one of your arms (right) under the right side of the down man underneath the elbow. Then place the wrist joint on the top of the head, pry up your opponent's arm, and drive your arm through, encircling his head. Be sure to squeeze the head. The free arm should be placed in the crotch to stabilize the down man.

Cradles: A cradle is an effective hold in which you literally cradle your opponent's head and leg in your arms. You accomplish this by driving a knee and the head of the opponent together. To be effective, the cradle must be tight.

Back cradle: This hold is an effective counter to a sit-out. Suppose the down wrestler sits out on you. As he does, you must control and stop him from completing the sit-out. To do this, press on his upper body and drive his head toward the mat. Then come off to the left side of the down man (you can maneuver to either side). Place your right elbow behind his neck. Grab his near arm just above the elbow—the most effective spot. Pull the elbow across his chest. With your left arm, scoop under his near leg and bring your hands together, locking with one of the following grips: (*a*) wrestler's grip; (*b*) palm lock; (*c*) hand on wrist. At the same time, push your right leg, which is bent under the lower hip, tight against his buttocks. Gently, but firmly, bring

Back cradle

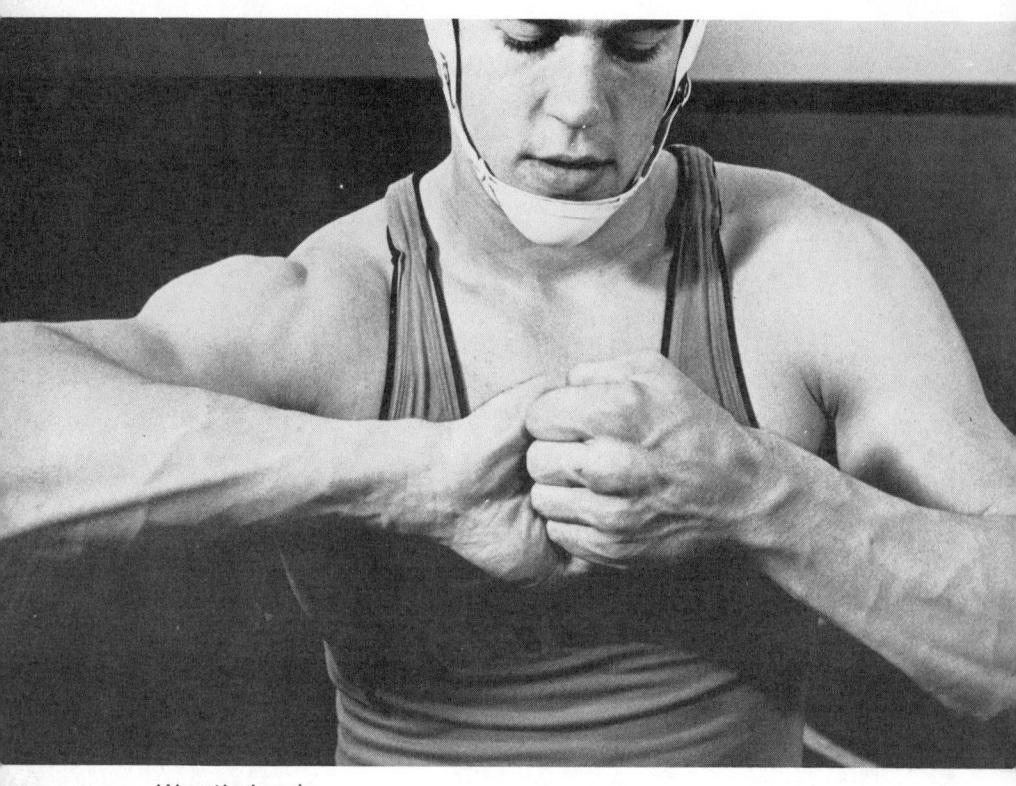

Wrestler's grip
Palm lock

CONTROL AND PINNING COMBINATIONS 107

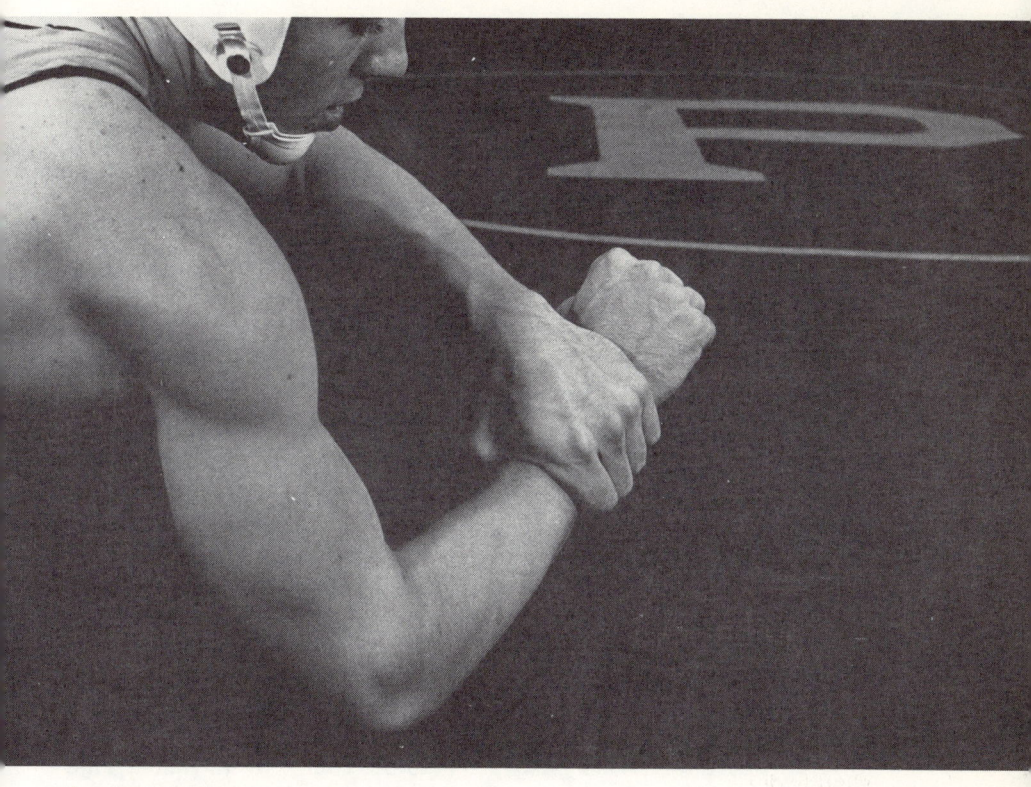

Hand on wrist

him back over your leg. Do you see what you have done? You elevated his hips as you brought his back close to the mat.

Once you feel you have good control, bring him again to his back. While you do this, you want to be on your right side so that your back will be nearly but not exactly, perpendicular to the mat. Drive your forehead into his temple so that your right arm, when it is locked around his head, pressures his carotid artery. Bend his head against your forearm. He can no longer bridge because you control his head. This hold reduces squirming and most upper body movement and aids you in holding those shoulders down for the required time. If he squirms and gets his shoulder up on your chest, stick your near knee into his hip and force it away.

A *straight cradle* is a variation of the back cradle. You have broken your man to his far side with a far arm and a far leg. If you hold his right extremities, you can maneuver for a half nelson. Scoop the top leg and cradle the knee and the head. The bottom man starts to turn toward

Leg split cradle

his front base and this is exactly what you want. If you have a long arm, you may want to cradle by grabbing your own wrist. If your arms are short, you will probably employ the *wrestler's grip*. When you gain that grip and bring his head and his knee together, pull your hands in toward your chest. This pulling will force your elbows just a little closer, maybe only 2 or 3 inches, but that means tighter control in the cradle. Drive diagonally to the opponent's down shoulder. Look toward his head and use your own head as a base on the far side.

Leg split cradle: This cradle is the same as the straight cradle with a slightly different finish-off. After you get your opponent on his side and have the cradle locked, step over his top leg with your right leg; pull the head toward that knee. Remember to keep constant pressure on the head toward the lower extremities to prevent him from regaining a base. Once you have stepped over his top leg with your right leg, step over it with your other leg and drive his calf up into your midsection. After you have stepped over it with your left leg, incline your leg and make sure you elevate it. Then walk around the head of the down man. This drives him onto his back, causes strain and pain, but immobilizes him for the required time.

Bridge over cradle: First, work a straight cradle. Often when you work a straight cradle the down wrestler will try to sit in toward you and recradle. When he sits on his buttocks and gets his head in the air, he has an effective base and has created problems for you. Bury your forehead in his hip, right into the flabby tissue in the bend above the

Bridge over cradle: opponent turning in

Bridge over cradle: burying your forehead

Bridge over cradle: bridging to high leg over

hip bone. With your forehead there, your next move is a high leg over into a bridge to force his back toward the mat. With your forehead still tucked into his hip, pull him toward you again and perform a second high leg over. As you do, step the far leg over the near leg and meet the down man chest to chest. Your lock on his head will have tightened up. Just before you take the second high leg over, be certain to pull his head hard back toward you. Your subsequent leg movement will exert a vise on his head, which is caught between your side and your biceps, and will shut off any bridging or turning by him. You will have also settled both of his shoulders securely to the mat.

Anytime your opponent's head is near his knee, as, for instance, when he steps up with an inside leg so that the leg is near his head, you can execute the *near side cradle*. Place your elbow (left) hand over his head, resting the elbow joint on the back of his neck. Place your chest on his side, rather than on his back. Remove your right hand from his waist and transfer it under and between his knees. Lock your hands in front of his chest. Your right elbow must be hooked at his knee, left elbow at his neck. After securing the lock, make sure his head goes down. Do not let him force his head up and sit through. To

CONTROL AND PINNING COMBINATIONS 111

force the head down, apply pressure toward you and down. Step up with your rear leg to gain a base for driving, then circle him, moving right, turning him as you pull his head down. When you circle, you take him off his base. Circling also allows you to set him on his back. If you were to drive him to his side instead, he could fight to stay off his shoulder.

If his head is not near his knee and you want to get a cradle, take his elbow hand by reaching up over his head and forcefully bringing it down behind his neck.

The *far side cradle* is used when he steps up with his far leg and leaves his head down. To lock up this cradle from a referee's position, bring the elbow hand over his head, and lock the waist hand around his far knee. Your lock is in front of the chest as it was in the near side cradle. To finish off, tighten up the cradle by forcing the lock to your chest. The most critical step is to turn under the man. The lock must stay tight. Put your right knee on the mat alongside his right knee. That stabilizes his down knee on the far side. As you rotate your body, pull the lock tight to your chest and roll under him on the far side. Keep in mind that moving the right arm all the way across to lock up is a dangerous maneuver, but if you remember your keys—lock tight to your chest, block the knee, roll under—you should not have a problem.

Far side cradle

Far side cradle

The *bow and arrow cradle* is good against an opponent who stays flat and protects himself by keeping his elbows in and legs together so that he is hard to turn over. Place your elbow hand on top of his head, index finger next to his ear. This gives you good position with your hand. You don't want to be too far up on his head or too far down on his neck, but right in the middle. Drop the other hand back to his near knee and bridge on the short rib of his near side. As you add pressure to his ribs with your forehead, you force him to buckle into you. As he turns, drive with your head away and pull his head and knee toward you, locking·up and continuing your drive to force him down.

To secure a *cross-face cradle,* drive your head and free arm to his leg. Post your hand on the mat behind the knee on his far side and crank him up, head to far knee. When close enough to lock, secure the lock and finish off. Pull his leg and head to your chest, and bring him back toward you. As you do, sometimes his back is not flat to the mat. To push him down, place your down knee in his hip joint, between the midsection of the hip and the thigh, and pull. Tighten up the cradle by placing your forehead on his temple and driving there and at the knee, pulling toward you with your lock.

Whenever you crank him up and he counters by sitting, withdraw the hand you had posted, hook his near arm to your chest, drive his

CONTROL AND PINNING COMBINATIONS

Cross-face cradle

Cross-face cradle: bringing opponent back into your lap

cross-face arm across his chest, and force him to his back for a cross-face pancake.

The *Turk cradle* is similar to the near side cradle except you finish it off differently. After securing the cradle lock, lift up his leg, step over the down leg with your near leg and hook. Extend your leg back so that you can hook his down leg at the heel. Raise your hips over his head; then drop your hip to the mat just above his head. Extend his Turked leg by placing your foot down on the mat, putting tremendous pressure on the sciatic nerve. If you do not get enough pressure push your midsection into his head, up under, forcing him onto his buttocks, and, at the same time, pull down with your lock and with the foot you have hooked.

One final point on cradles: Your opponent's head has to be down and you must have a good lock. If you lose the lock, you lose the cradle.

The next pinning combination is a **navy ride** (also called a *lace ride*). To get into the navy ride, take the waist and far ankle. Pull the leg up onto your thigh. At the same time, step up on your foot, which you have placed between your opponent's feet. Reach down over the top leg under his bottom knee to the opposite shoulder. Take the lock at the knee.

You can get into the same situation if he works a sit-out. Just take your front arm across and hook under his far knee. If you come in from the right side, take the right arm, hook the down knee, keep your free hand around the waist, pick up on the knee, and bring it diagonally across to the far shoulder. When you do that, the opponent rocks to his back flat on the mat. If he fights violently to the down side—the best side to fight to—expect him to turn in, then hit him with chest pressure, a bar arm, or even a half nelson.

The safest way to fight out of a navy ride is to fight away. If he fights away and reaches with his arms, then you should back hook the arm and lift at the knee. If he fights so hard that it is too tough to let go or free your hand, then lock your hands. Gain some leverage by sticking your elbow in his sternum. Pick up the lock, again toward your chest, either down or up to his far shoulder. Look for a half nelson or possibly a cradle.

The **bar arm** and the **hook series:** For the bar arm series, let's put your opponent down in the referee's position. Move your elbow hand from the outside to the front of his arm. Bring up your hand under the armpit, then place it on his back. Lock his near arm above the elbow. Apply forward pressure and drive him flat, destroying his base. When you barred the arm, you took out one of the four points in his table.

Cross-face cradle

Turk cradle

Turk cradle finish-off

If you cannot take the arm, rise up on your toes and run him forward, applying all your weight down to keep his arm locked in a bar. From this bar, after you get him flat, you try to immobilize the far or down arm. You can do this any number of ways. We will cover two of them.

1. Place your hand on the mat on the outside of his hand. That stabilizes the retreat or the advancement of that arm.

2. Try for a one-on-one on the downside wrist. Then transfer pressure at a cross angle from the near hip through to the far shoulder. Keep your chest low and that arm as high on your chest as you can. Bulldoze him from the near hip through to the far shoulder. Put your inside knee right into his face and drive him as far forward as you can. Kick your trailing leg, the top leg, all the way over him, letting go of the one-on-one on the downside arm. Once you have applied that much pressure there is no way he can adjust his downside. As soon as you have pinned him down, jam your knee toward his face. Kick your top leg 180 degrees over him and force his back onto the mat. From here, look for a half nelson or for any kind of head control.

As soon as they gain a bar arm and the one-on-one on the far side, wrestlers who have more flexibility and very long arms, can pull the down arm in while they kick, then lock their hands and take the man

CONTROL AND PINNING COMBINATIONS

Back hook

over behind their backs. By trapping both arms, you create a real predicament for your opponent. Not every wrestler can maintain his balance once he takes his man over; that is why most wrestlers will release on the downside. Once you get your man over to his back, hold the bar arm, look for a check, and come over the head with the free arm and under the neck with a lock or a half nelson, depending upon the direction that your opponent turns.

We can describe a **double arm bar series** where you would have a bar on the inside and a bar on the outside. Lock your hands and take the man in either direction. If he pressures you from one side, then step up to the opposite side, go around the head and drive him to his side, pulling the arm in. Once you get the man to his side—in most situations he will be near his back—lock around the hands and sit through. This forces even more pressure on the arms, and makes it almost impossible for the man to do anything except suffer extreme pain.

Hooks: Whenever your opponent sits out or whenever he is on his side and posts an arm on the outside or top side, he is susceptible to hooks. To hook an opponent, wedge your thumb and index finger between his side and arm and hook him at the elbow.

Here is a good hook situation: Break the man to his side. He posts his top arm so you hook under his elbow, placing your hand on top of his elbow and pulling it behind his back. Keep your hook arm perpendicular to the mat. The palm of your hand comes under, then up on top of the elbow. Block the head with your down leg in front of his face, then kick over your trailing leg. Transfer from a hook and go around his head into a bar and a half or a bar and head lock.

Stay with your hook and enter into a double underhook, transferring into a bar on the inside. From the hook, you can also go to a double hook. Once you have a double hook, release the waist hand and transfer into a bar; pull the chin back, lock behind the man's neck, or stay with a half nelson. Instead of transferring into a bar, you can hook, block the head with your free hand, and pull the man back. He is going to fight to his belly. His top leg will extend so you can go around the front again and this time hit the knee with your free hand and throw it straight up in the air. This action turns his shoulders to the mat. From here, catch any purchase you can. You have the hook; go around and throw the knee, then look for a bar arm and transfer to a half nelson. Or, look for a crotch pry. The hook and bar series work hand in hand.

CONTROL AND PINNING SITUATIONS USING THE LEGS

An expert wrestler who is also proficient with his legs is a formidable opponent. Legs are also a great equalizer because an individual can compensate against a stronger wrestler if he has powerful and agile legs. The power in the legs is potentially much greater than that in the upper body. On the other hand, a good leg wrestler must be well skilled in the other holds for he cannot rely on legs alone.

There are three important factors in successful leg wrestling: (1) You must have elevation for leverage. Your head, hips, and main body weight must be on the down man so that you make him carry your weight. (2) Keep the down wrestler between you and the mat. Too

Cross-body ride

many times in leg wrestling a leg man will lose his control because the defensive wrestler obtains height and maneuvers the attacker between him and the mat. (3) Square your hips to the man so that he is controlled, even when you are at his side or on top of him or underneath momentarily.

The top man can use leg rides to turn the down man over to his back.

The cross-body ride is gained by attacking under your man's belly driving a leg between his legs, then hooking the foot on his lower leg. Your upper body should be well over his back and your free leg bent perpendicular to the long axis of his body. You have removed one of the legs of his table.

Another way to get into the cross-body ride is to block out your opponent's inside elbow so he does not pick up your leg as it comes in. Push it forward and drive the man sideways, perpendicular to his long axis to open up the inside leg. Put your leg in and again lock the lower leg.

Turk ride with head control

A third way to get the cross-body ride is to extend the leg with the bulldog ride, driving the man perpendicular again, sticking the down leg in between your opponent's legs, and locking your foot around his lower leg.

Once you learn the cross-body ride, drill with a partner to learn how to maintain the cross-body ride when the bottom man moves.

Learn, too, how to transfer from the cross to a **Jacob's ride,** which can be turned into a pin. From the cross body, swing the free leg in a long arc toward your opponent's back and over the far side. Your man will collapse on the far side. From the side position, bar his top arm. Come over, lock on the arm above the elbow, and drive your elbow down onto the mat next to his ear. That tightens up his upper body. At the same time, knees and heels come together and form a tent to prevent him from freeing his legs. Not only do you have the *Jacob's hook* (sometimes referred to as the *bar arm and Jacob's ride*), but you also can attack his head, locking your free arm—your inside arm— around his head and bringing his shoulders back to the mat. Place your hand on the far side of his head, pull it toward his near shoulder, then turn his face down, to eliminate his chance of bridging and to stabilize his upper body.

To get into a **Turk ride** from the referee's position, pull the inside leg to open up a clear shot to the far knee. Step in with the inside leg

CONTROL AND PINNING COMBINATIONS

behind the far knee. After you have planted that foot, swan dive across the man. Once you get to the far side, scoop up the heel, and again, with heels together, tent your legs, arch your back, and post your hands on the mat to give yourself plenty of height. From here, you can bar the top arm, or, again, use the same kind of head control that you worked in the Jacob's.

Once you learn the Jacob's and the Turk, learn how to transfer back and forth. Simply go into the Turk first. The man turns away. You transfer into the Jacob's by sliding parallel to the man and getting a bar arm on his top arm. He turns in and then you can transfer again. Go perpendicular and bar the other arm, which now is the top arm. Hook the leg in the same manner. The bottom man's reaction of turning in provides you the chance to transfer from a Jacob's to a Turk or from a Turk to a Jacob's.

After you have learned these two moves, return to a cross-body ride. The bottom man sits out, the top man goes right into a Jacob's; the bottom man turns in, the top man transfers into a Turk; bottom man turns out, top man transfers into a Jacob's; bottom man continues and goes up to his base, and the top man comes up to a cross-body ride.

Guillotine: This is one of the most effective and punishing pins in the series of leg rides. From the cross-body ride, place your free leg perpendicular to your man to provide balance to that side. Place your elbow behind his armpit to give you stability on the far side. Pull or force your elbow to your side, forcing weight to the far side or actually onto the inside arm. The far arm is now light. Reach down with both hands, grab the arm below the elbow, and pull it tight to your chest. Once you have pulled it to your chest, control the wrist with your far

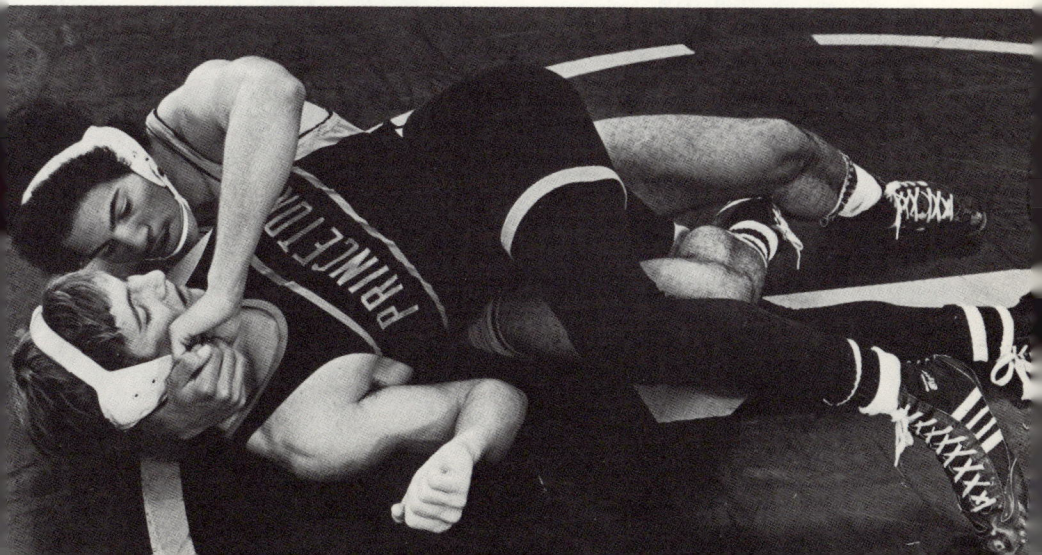

Guillotine from cross-body control

arm (your right arm). Pull it over your head and keep the elbow in his armpit. Drive and torque your upper body, thrusting your left elbow into his back. Grab his head, lock around it, and slowly take him to his back. Once you get him to that position, extend your grapevine leg, shoot your hips into him, and pull his head toward you. This produces heavy pressure on his body.

Sometimes your man might lock and pull your head down to the far side. As long as you have the elbow in front of his shoulder, you are in good shape. Collapse on the far side, roll under, and as soon as you do your elbow has to drive to the mat. Your leg extends. With the leg straight, and the elbow driving back, you should never get caught under the man. When you roll under, you will come out on top and your opponent will be on his back. After you have driven your elbow to the mat, pick up the head, lock around it, and secure a tight position. On occasion, your foot will come free of his lower leg. Do not be upset if this occurs. With your free leg, keep the foot that is grapevined in the crotch, step over the foot with your free leg, and figure 4 it (tuck the foot of the free leg under the knee of your other leg). Do not worry about holding the leg. It is helpful if you have it. You can extend it, but

Cross-body ride with cross-face pinning combination

CONTROL AND PINNING COMBINATIONS

if you lose foot control on the lower leg, you can figure 4 your own leg, let's say your right leg, by just stepping over the left leg and forming the figure 4.

The **cross face** is another leg-pinning combination from the cross-body ride. Instead of driving in behind the armpit with the elbow, drive the head to the far arm. Lock above the elbow. Pull that arm into your opponent's body, then pull him to his back. You have that arm barred and can drive your hips into him, locking your hands around the far arm and executing a double arm bar. Finish off with a high arch of your midsection into his back, extending the leg and locking around both arms. This is a very effective and tight pin.

4

General Defensive Positions

A wrestler must have good offense to score points, but he must also be sound defensively. There are several principles of good defense. The best defense is to employ an effective offense. Do not wait for your opponent to move, but initiate your own move. Have a good stance and be prepared to move in any direction in reaction to your opponent's motions. Hand movement is critical—tips of the fingers to tips of the elbows. Use the hands to ward off attempts at control by your opponent. Keep your elbows near your side to prevent duck-unders or leg attacks. Body motion is essential, too. Move around in an unpredictable manner so that you are a more difficult target.

LINES OF DEFENSE

The first line of defense against an attack is the hands. The attacker must always penetrate your hands first. The second line of defense is the hips. If the attacker comes low, lower the boom on him. That means throw your legs and feet back or sprawl, and drop your hips into him, putting your weight and pressure on his arms and shoulders. Dropping back forces him higher on your body and reduces his effectiveness.

There are two general tactics in defense when you are wrestling an opponent on your feet, or in the neutral position. The conventional way to ward off a leg attack is to lower the boom. The Olympic, or freestyle, stresses bumping your opponent with your hips, then immediately firing right back with an offensive move of your own. This second tactic is better suited for a more experienced wrestler.

GENERAL DEFENSIVE POSITIONS　　　　　　　　　　　125

DEFENSING NEUTRAL POSITION ATTACKS

There are several ways to counter leg attacks. In general, it is important after your opponent shoots and makes contact that you *adjust* your position. To finish off a single-leg attack, the opponent will try to angle off. Your best defense is to stay square with him: Try to keep your hips perpendicular to him and his base stationary as you adjust to his motion. At the same time, ward him off with your hands. We refer to this simple counter as **adjustment.**

Expansion: Whenever an offensive wrestler locks around your single leg, make him lock at your knee. A lock at the knee is easier to

Expansion to counter single-leg attack

defend than one above or below the knee. If he locks the knee, overhook him on the side closest to you, then grab his far wrist—overhook on the inside and wrist control on the outside. Expand your leg sporadically and violently to force his hands down and simultaneously jerk the arms apart. Both moves have to be explosive to break the lock. Once it is broken, square off with your opponent and look for an offensive attack.

Stepping over: Whenever an attacker shoots in on a single leg below the knee, the first thing you do to stabilize him is square off and drive your knee into his shoulder. Then, reverse-step over him.

Suppose he attacks your right leg: Concede the leg he has attacked and step with your left leg over his back. Once you step over him, watch for a chance to initiate offense from this countermaneuver. The controlled leg now vices the back of his neck. Maintain your height and pressure his shoulder downward. Pick behind the near knee and drive him across onto his side, then keep the leg and use a figure 4 on his head and shoulder. If you take your man to his back, keep the figure 4 with ankle or knee control and you will not only get control points but possibly some back points as well. On the other hand, if your opponent maintains tight control of your leg and you are unable to throw him to his back or side, and have locked into the crotch, a stalemate will probably be called. In essence, you have countered a single-leg attempt by producing a stalemate.

We want to point out that from the stepover position, you can also use a **waistlock and bump.** Reverse the bodylock and bump your opponent to his side. Finish off your reverse stepover by picking up that near knee and stepping into a Turk ride, knocking him to his side with your free legs and smacking your heels together to break his lock on the single leg. If you can execute the stepover into the Turk and get your heels together, you should get a 2-point takedown. From there, look for a bar arm or head or upper body control for bonus back points.

Reverse bodylock: Your opponent attacks your left leg. Instead of going to the overhook with your left arm, go under his stomach across his body and sprawl. Try to post him and stabilize him with your hips. You don't want him to penetrate or get his head high or his knees up under his chest. With the reverse bodylock, throw him to his far side. It takes a good effort. Move your hips clockwise, work his knees closer together to knock him off his base. Once you get him to his side, spin around his head counterclockwise toward his back. As you go around, pull out your hand.

Stepping over head as defense to single leg

Waistlock and knee bump

High leg over to cradle

The **head drag:** When your opponent attacks the single leg, drive your hips into him and meet him head-on to stop penetration. Grab his chin with the left hand, use the right hand as a reinforcer, and push his head outside. With his head outside, he is vulnerable to a near-arm drag. Grab behind the elbow of the near arm and stop him from retreating. Spin around behind him so that the arm or elbow hook can either be a drag or a stabilizer. With your free hand, go to the deep crotch, but remember, whenever you go behind a man, check the crotch or far ankle. It is not wise to go around his waist.

High leg over: Your opponent attacks your left leg and you lower the boom to stabilize him. Work parallel to him and force his upper body down with an overhook. Using the forward force of the overhook, break him to his side, flat. Keeping the overhook in, put the palm of your hand on the mat as a pivot and step over his back with your far leg. Your near leg is across his stomach or leg. Your far leg braces to push you back toward your opponent. The next move is a cradle. Out comes the pivot arm and around his neck it goes. Your far arm scoops up his near knee and you have cradled him right around your leg. If you miss the cradle, he will usually go to a front base, allowing you to move on top into a controlling position.

180-degree turn: When your opponent has a single leg up in the air, the higher he gets that single leg, the more uncomfortable it is for you and the harder it is to get free. You can do one of two things:

1. If he has the left leg high, face toward him as much as possible and then turn away from him, propelling your upper body 180 degrees

GENERAL DEFENSIVE POSITIONS

and land on your hands. As you land, try to whip your leg by pulling it to your chest. Once that knee comes to your chest and your foot hits the mat, you cannot stay there or he will drop down on top of you. Propel yourself forward until you are sure you can turn and face him.

2. A second move against your opponent's single-leg lift is to tuck your chin to your chest, then drop down between his legs, landing on your shoulder. Don't land on the top of your head. The farther back you are on your shoulder, the better you will be. Your momentum drives him forward. Raise your head and bring your back up in the air, then come out the back door, through his legs, up behind him.

180-degree turn

Head drive: Once the attacker starts his penetration, push your palms against his head to open distance between him and you. Push in the opposite direction from the way he wants to go. If he overextends his base, reach over his back with your right hand, grab his far ankle at the instep, and pull it into his buttocks. That puts pressure on his forehead, forcing it toward the mat. Change your hand from the side to the top of his head and drive his head to the mat. Release the ankle and place that arm over his upper arm, then under his armpit and across the front of his shoulder locking on the wrist that is driving down his head—this is a **quarter nelson.**

The immediate reaction of the attacker, when he feels his head going down, is to thrust his head up and get his knee under. You have the quarter nelson in, so at the same time you drive down his head, sprawl slightly and drive your hip in toward him to block him off. Bent from head to hip, your body should form an angle of 120 degrees. As he starts to bring his head up and his knees under his chest, assist him by lifting with your arm under his shoulder to force that shoulder straight up. Slide your knee next to his near knee and plant it. Now straighten him up so that you are chest to chest. His knee becomes the point of rotation. Chest to chest, near knee against near knee, trailing knee off the deck, plant your foot, rotate directly in toward him, and keep a tight grip with the overhooked arm. As you do this, you force him off his base toward his back. Follow through with the free arm, cutting across his chest and taking him to the mat. When you meet him on the mat, keep the overhook and apply pressure upward by grabbing behind his tricep with the overhook arm. Lift up this arm, meet him chest to chest and disperse your weight across his upper body. You have executed a **pancake** and should get credit for a takedown and back points.

A second offensive maneuver from a quarter nelson is to lift his upper body off the mat. As you come off your knees, propel him in a circle. As his upper body stretches out away from its base, use your overhook arm to extend him. He should fall flat. Then jump on top. If, as you start to throw-by, he locks your underhooked or overhooked arm then come back into a quick drag. As you drag the elbow to your side, pull him off his base. Because of motion and the elongated position of his body, he can no longer retain his balance.

A third line of offense is to drive his head with the quarter nelson into the mat. Let's assume he does not try to straighten out. He may try to control your hand on his head. As you drove his head, you cleared yourself of him and pushed him down with your left hand. Now place your left knee against his head and push his head into your knee. Pull off the pushing hand and reach into his rear crotch. Pull that rear crotch in toward your lap. With his head stabilized, his knees cannot keep a base.

The **cross-face opposite arm** is especially good against the double leg. Keep your hips square with him. Drive your index finger of the hand on the same side as his head across the bridge of his nose. This forces away his head. Continue driving his head and secure a lock on the far arm above the elbow. With his face turned, you have an easier grab on the arm. You now have a purchase on his body. Maneuver your hips side to side and withdraw your body from his.

Suppose your opponent gets through your first line of defense, the hands. Lower the boom and overhook him. The overhook stabilizes his one side. It helps you stop his penetration and allows you to throw back your legs or hips. Keep driving your hips side to side away from him to keep his lock off your double leg. When he feels the increased weight of your body he will drop the lock or his arms off your legs and try to maintain a base.

COUNTERING UPPER BODY ATTACKS

Elbow control: Remember that most wrestlers are taught to gain inside control. As the defensive wrestler, you don't really need inside control. Let your opponent control your collar. The first thing you do is control the elbow that has your collar. Lift his elbow to alleviate the pressure of his forearm. Then work for elbow control on the other side to shut off the chance of his trying an upper body takedown.

A second simple counter to an upper body attack is an **elbow hook.** He has your collar on an inside tie-up. Instead of overtying his collar as you would to set up a duck under or shrug, overtie his arm and hook the inside of his elbow with a *fishhook*. With your other (right) hand, lift his elbow to immobilize his two arms from elbows to fingertips. Any forward motion by him must now come through your arms.

Over-and-under tie: When he ties you up on the inside of your collar—let's say the left side of your neck—grab his arm underneath his tricep with your left arm. Instead of tying his collar, go behind his neck and lock your hand in a wrestler's grip. What do you do with your head? In a neutral tie-up neither man should be any deeper than forehead to forehead. Sometimes by accident you get in tight. As you bend him over, push your head into his neck and pull his head toward you. This is a general body tie, a temporary position that shuts off his offense until you can generate your own offense.

Barrel-roll tie: Move into a barrel-roll tie with a collar and bicep tie-up. Just as in the barrel roll, it is most important to control the elbow of his controlling arm. Pull this elbow against your shoulder as you thrust your head under that same arm. Your other hand on his collar now encircles his waist or blocks off his chest or hip. With the one arm tied very tightly, bend over about 45 degrees, flexing your knees if need be.

The **Russian tie** is one of the best defenses against an opponent who attacks on his feet. If you can take away one of his arms with a Russian tie-up, you have eliminated much of his offense since he cannot easily perform an offensive maneuver on his feet with only one arm. It is almost impossible to initiate a takedown with one arm.

The **underhook** shuts off many of the offensive maneuvers that your opponent can use if he controls your upper body. Block out the far shoulder because the underhook makes you vulnerable to a wrestler who uses a high crotch. Generally, the only time your opponent will initiate a high crotch is if he has the far side shoulder free. He will concede one arm if he can get his other arm and shoulder down under your crotch. How do you stop that? In your underhook, one side blocks out any attack. Your free hand blocks the shoulder or strives for wrist or elbow control to prevent your opponent from going under with his free arm. If you don't have good control on the free side, you are susceptible to the high crotch. Today's wrestlers use the high crotch more and more effectively.

Overtie and block: This maneuver is especially good against an attack to the upper body from a collar tie-up. If your opponent ties up your collar, his left hand on your right side, simply come over from the outside with your right hand, the hand on the same side he tied up, and block him on his chin or neck, preferably on the chin. Drive his head away and block out any attack. Sometimes you can even put your thumb at the base of his neck and drive him with your shoulder, keeping him at bay and not allowing him to control any collar tie-up.

DEFENSING BOTTOM OFFENSE

Countering stand-ups: Once the down man gains his feet, it is important that you maintain body contact and control his hips. Keep your chest on the back of his hips. Do not let him create space bet-

GENERAL DEFENSIVE POSITIONS

Controlling opponent's far elbow to counter Russian arm control

ween his hips and your chest. Once he has stood up, he is fighting for hand control. Press a forearm on either one of his legs—for example, the left leg. Your head is on the same side as the down pressure. Drive your left leg into his Achilles tendon—don't kick or injure him. Turn your instep to block his heel from moving and step with the right leg to force a circular motion. As you step, pull him to his left hip. Before his hip hits the mat, place your right knee in his crotch. This is a *backheel counter.*

Two common mistakes here are allowing space to open between the two bodies, and pulling your opponent directly on top of you as he falls. With your right knee in his crotch, carry him through as he hits. Your momentum propels you right up on top of him.

Another counter for a stand-up is a *butt drive.* Assume he is on his feet and you are losing your grip. Slide your hands down his side and hold him just above the knees. Drop to your knees, get your shoulder under his buttocks, then drive him forward. The pressure on his knees stabilizes his legs and he cannot walk away from you. Drive your shoulder upward into his buttocks and straighten him. He will lose his balance and fall.

If you find yourself losing control with your hand, another resourceful move is the *ankle lift.* Recognize quickly that you cannot keep your hands interlocked, then drop them to the nearest ankle. Circle that ankle with both of your arms tightly and quickly; next, raise the ankle to your chest. Do not let him balance on that down leg, but move him and continue to lift up and sweep. Make him hop as you lift upward and destroy his base.

Leg pressure: Perhaps you did not get his ankle as high as you wanted, or he stopped you. Put his heel on the thigh of your outside leg. Try to stabilize that heel with your far arm and reinforce it with your near leg. Slide up the leg toward his knee, grabbing his shinbone just below the knee and adding more pressure across his shin. He no longer has any foot to brace himself and falls to his hip.

Knee elevator and trip: When you have his leg at the ankle, he might bend his knee before you get the leg high enough and start to work his leg in toward you, gaining an overhook at the same time. Let's assume he has a wrist overhook. Move him off his base, lift your far leg so your thigh or knee hits underneath his heel. This elevates his leg so that you can stick your far arm under his heel, lodging the heel in the crook of your elbow. Turn him clockwise to force him backwards and knock out his base leg with your near foot.

Leg lace and cross pressure: You can counter a tripod by first

Elevating knee to gain height

Leg lace and low cross pressure

bulldogging the near leg, then hooking your opponent's far hip with your waist hand. Shove your head into his stomach, keeping the leg hooked at the ankle. Place your free arm across and in front of his far leg behind the Achilles tendon and pull his hip back, using the cross pressure of the leg hook and your head to drive him backward.

Two-on-one with a front trip: When your opponent tries to stand up, pull his near arm into his side. With your arm around the waist, control a single wrist. With the far arm on his elbow, you have a two-on-one. Using the two-on-one, as your opponent tries to stand, stabilize his base and then step across in front of him and trip him forward. As you fall toward the mat, let go of the elbow and brace as you hit the mat so that he cannot roll you.

Crotch lift: Suppose the down wrestler stands and you have had a hard time controlling his hips. A little space has opened between his hips and your chest. With one arm still around his waist, lock into the crotch with your free arm, hook up the waist arm, and lift. The crotch lift causes him pain.

Body lift: Assume that the down wrestler has freed his arms and you cannot control either arm. Lower your base slightly, setting under his

Two-on-one with a front trip

GENERAL DEFENSIVE POSITIONS

buttocks, and pull him in tightly to your waist. Now you are ready to lift him, but make sure your lift is high. When you are ready to set him down—this is critical—you have to remove one of his leverage points. Assume that your head and the major part of your body are on the down wrestler's left side. As you start to set him down, block his near leg with your far (left) leg to prevent him from establishing a base or blocking his fall. Be ready for a roll. Spread yourself out and cover your man thoroughly once you hit the mat.

Double-leg lift: As the down man stands and tries to gain hand control, he will also want to turn into the top wrestler. Do not release him but bait him a little and let him begin to turn in toward you. As he does, move your far arm, which was hooking his near elbow, across and behind the thigh of your opponent. As he continues to turn toward you, meet him with your shoulder in his stomach and your waist arm behind his near leg. The situation is similar to a double leg. Pick him up in the air and move your near arm from the outside crotch to the inside. With the far arm, throw in a half nelson and set him down on the near shoulder.

Double-leg lift

Countering a sit-out: Against a *long sit-out*, maintain some control around the waist and sit out yourself, following in the same direction as your opponent so that you wind up in the position that you started. If your opponent beats you to his sit-out and turns before you can sit out behind him, hook his arm with the arm that was around his waist and go behind him in an opposite direction. If you are in a conventional starting position, when he steps out to the right and turns back toward you, hook his right arm with your right arm, then go behind to the left rather than to the right.

Against the *short sit-out*, drive your chest down and keep your head over the midline of his back. Do not put your head to one side or the other because you then set up another offensive maneuver—the *head grab and check*. Apply pressure with your forehead in the midline of his back and drive his head down to his knees. If you can do that you have also set him up for a cradle to either side. If you are unable to get his head down near his knees and maintain the forward pressure, bring your arms outside from both sides, and pry in on his crotch or the inside of both thighs. Remember, if he gains wrist control, immediately go to cross control. If he controls your right wrist, then you must

Cross-wrist control

GENERAL DEFENSIVE POSITIONS

control his control with your free hand. This is referred to as *cross wrist control* or *cross control*. If your opponent gets under one of your arms you immediately have to shift and try to gain control to that side. You can also drive forward, then slip out to the front and pick up an ankle, forcing it up and driving his shoulders to the mat. The higher the ankle control, the easier it is to control your man.

Counters against rolls: To shut off side or wing rolls, maintain a right angle to the bottom man and press your upper body weight heavily on your opponent's side. Keep your opponent's knees together and put weight on them whenever he attempts to elevate. The more parallel to him you are, the more susceptible you will be to a side or wing roll. If you are too high, it is best to go to the opposite side or to the same side he has your wrist.

You can cut off *shoulder rolls* and *bridge rolls* with proper position. A bar arm, rear crotch, or one-on-one and rear crotch can prevent the shoulder roll. If you are on top, keep your opponent's head buried in the mat and his hips jacked up. A lot of weight must be upon your man's shoulders. Stay at a right angle. Again, when wrestling on top, your chances of controlling the bottom man are greatly enhanced if you ride perpendicular to him.

Hand control from the bottom: This is simply cross control. When your opponent uses any type of hand control—as an offensive maneuver from the bottom, you can kill his hand control with cross control.

Countering the switch: Whenever your man tries to switch, control his waist tightly and keep your shoulder close to him so you can control the hips. To stop him from executing his switch, hold your head high and off the mat. Put your ear or head right between your opponent's shoulder blades. That helps you to maintain your height, which is critical, and also gives you a better sense of where your man is going as he attempts his switch. If your head drops to the mat, you will almost invariably be reversed with the switch. If he continues around with his switch, go behind him and maintain control of his hips from the rear. If you drop your head and are unable to get it back up and he starts to go around with his switch, as soon as he raises his hips off the deck you must reswitch or sit back under him and execute the same maneuver against him that he has just done against you. Switch and reswitch but only after you have totally committed yourself and have dropped your head.

Sometimes you are not able to get a reswitch or your man keeps his hips low. Then push yourself back and step over him all the way to the far side. When you do this, he often returns to his base because now he is in the awkward position of lying on his back.

Another counter is a simple *limp arm*. This requires precise timing. When your opponent initiates the switch, offer a limp arm and then shoot for a far ankle. When he initiates the switch, circle wide, drop your shoulder, and pull out the waist arm. If, in fact, you have no arm around the waist, it is impossible for him to complete a switch because there is no post on which he can arch back and apply the leverage and pressure that is needed in a switch.

DEFENSING TOP OFFENSE

Tight waist: If the top man executes a tight waist and it is hard for you to get out of it, jam your hips back into his waist. Crowd him and keep jamming, forcing, and pushing your feet. Try to rise into a sitting position, not exactly upright, but about 45 degrees or so, with your side to the mat. When you push your hips into him, he has to drive against you and then you can attempt to execute a *hip-heist switch*.

Counters to ankle checks: If your opponent is allowed to control your ankle when you are down, he will control you. Get your ankle free—that is your first essential task. You need your ankles to perform your own offensive maneuvers from the bottom. If he grabs the far ankle and waist, grab his wrist and plant the foot he controls. As soon as you do that, push back into him and force your hips between his chest and your foot. When you push back and stabilize the ankle on the mat, post the hand on the same side. With that hand posted, you have an effective offensive tool.

You can also kick your leg straight back to free the ankle.

Or, you can concede the ankle and attack the waist hand. Clear the hip of his waist hand. Then, step up with the leg on the same side that you have cleared the hip. To complete the escape, scoot away. Assume a sprinter's start position and leap forward as far as you can with a double hop. Turn and face your man.

If you know that your opponent is an ankle checker or an ankle rider, then as soon as the whistle blows, move your feet to a sitting position. If your ankles are out front, your opponent cannot check them. Sit on them and cover them. Rather than curl your toes, extend them and sit on your arches. Fight for hand control off the whistle and as soon as you have it on one side, step up to that side or curl your toes and start your offensive maneuver from the bottom so that your opponent does not have the chance to check your ankle.

Countering a bulldog: As we said earlier, the bulldog ride occurs when the top wrestler laces up the lower part of your near leg. Your natural reaction is to pull forward. The more you pull forward, the more secure your opponent, the top man, becomes and the more riding time he gains.

There are three pretty good counters for this bulldog ride. The first one is a *side roll.* In the bulldog ride, your opponent on top is parallel to you on the bottom. Jam with your near hip and back into him. Use your far arm to knock off his elbow hook. In most cases he will resist this. As he does, hook up the arm that is around your waist and proceed to a side roll. Fall down on your far side, using your elbow as a post for upper body elevation. It is then a matter of finishing off. Often, when a down wrestler has elevated the controlling wrestler to his side, the near leg of the down man will remain hooked. He has to free this leg. If he cannot, he braces it as a support and drives in toward his opponent to face him chest to chest.

A second method of countering a bulldog is to constantly jam your hips into him and drive him back onto his buttocks. This forces the knee of his hooking leg up. Your next move is to switch or sit out deep. Pull the knee of your hooked leg with every ounce of energy you have toward your chest. Nine times out of ten, you can free it this way.

The third method to break the bulldog is with an *overhook.* Move into the controlling wrestler with an overhook, applying downward pressure with your arm as you hit him with your near hip. Square off out in front for a 1-point neutral.

Countering overhooks: In an overhook, the more height a wrestler has the better he can either counter or finish off the overhook. A common fault is to drop low against an overhook. Stay high. You may have to post the hand on the outside initially but, to get good height, step up with the outside foot. When you do that, invariably your opponent will push into you. As he does, return the pressure, then rise up on your feet and read his position. If he leans forward, step under him, bear-hug his waist, and throw him. If he is straight up, put your head into his chest, buckle his inside knee with your inside knee, and take him to his back.

The second way to counter the overhook is to use a *limp arm.* Maintain your height. Now, if you have the height advantage your opponent will drive down. Loosen up the overhook pressure by first driving up and then giving way to his pressure down. At the same time,

Limp arm

turn your palm up on the arm that is overhooked and drop the shoulder down in a large circle. As you come back up after your arm is freed, go to a far ankle and ride. Do not, we emphasize, do not go back to the waist. If, after you limp arm your way out of the overhook, you go back to a waist ride, your opponent will recapture the overhook and your limp arm will have been in vain.

Another way to counter the overhook is the *drop-low and far-ankle drive*. Sink low on the inside leg and drop the arm that is around the waist into your opponent's crotch. Reach for the far ankle. If you can attack the far ankle then you can stabilize your opponent and drive him to his side. On his side, he is more concerned about self-preservation or staying off his back than attacking with the overhook.

The fourth counter to the overhook is the roll-through. Here it is important to control your man's far hip with a strong arm around his waist. Try to roll completely under him while you control that hip. As you go, block his far knee, pull at his hip and push on the far knee, rolling under him and into a position as he rolls over you onto his back. Do not go under him until you feel you have secure hip control.

A good way to set up this move is to drive until he starts to drive down. As soon as he presses, he is helping you with that down pressure. Initiate your roll under. As you go, block the far knee, then roll through and wind up on the top. Be aware that this is a dangerous maneuver if you do not have good wrist control. Anytime your man gives you sporadic pressure down, you can use this counter.

GENERAL DEFENSIVE POSITIONS

Double trouble. If your opponent overhooks you and drops his head, let him stay in the overhook. Rap him over the head with your free arm, pushing down his head and pulling it toward you in a manner similar to the method we used in a near side cradle. Lock you hand under the far armpit and force him to his back. Step up with your rear foot and drive him forward, tucking him under.

Counters from a prone position: The top wrestler has broken you to the mat. Your stomach is on the mat, your feet are straight out, you are as flat as a pancake. What do you do? First, establish a base before you think about escapes or reversals.

Suppose he controls your waist and has a near arm bar on your left side. Instead of lying flat, elevate to the greatest angle you can, 2 or 3 degrees, whatever you can get. As you do, bring your left knee up under your chest as much as possible. Push your hips back over your leg as far as you can. You create a space on your far (right) side. Once you have that space, bring the right knee up under your chest as much as possible. Push your hips back over your thighs to gain more elevation. By pushing and pulling and thereby creating these spaces, you eventually build a base. When you have created this base, and only then, you can begin to generate offense.

Countering legs off the bottom: Although a leg wrestler can be a formidable opponent, you can stop a leg wrestler by preventing him from gaining height and by keeping him between you and the mat to block off pressure from his hips. When you know you will face a leg wrestler, move quickly, sharply, stay compact, and keep your elbows close to your sides at all times. Regardless of how proficient he is with his legs, if you continue to be caught and trapped by legs you are reacting too slowly. An alert wrestler with explosive power will seldom get caught by leg wrestlers.

A simple *leg extension* is an effective counter. If you are in a four-point base and your opponent tries to hook your leg with his leg, just straighten your leg back, hip high, parallel with the mat.

To prevent a cross leg or a grapevine, keep your arms in front and your elbows near your side. (A grapevine or cross leg is a hold in which the offensive wrestler hooks his leg around the thigh and lower leg of the down wrestler. In a double-leg grapevine, the top man uses both legs in similar manner to control both legs of the down man.) Do not let the offensive wrestler capture one of your arms or else it will be harder for you to escape.

Knee lock and extension: Let's assume the top man has his leg hooked in, not deep. Keep a solid base, drop your forehead to the mat, and lock behind his cross leg at the hooked knee, locking your hands in a wrestler's grip. Stabilize his knee and extend your leg. He cannot retain the position without his leg hooked in.

You can counter a cross-leg ride with an *inside sit-out*. If the top man tries to hook your left leg, quickly sit on your left hip and throw your left leg toward your right hand. By doing this with sudden force, you straighten out the leg of the attacker. The next step is to use your far (right) arm to either pick off or scoop up under that cross-leg ride. As you perform one or the other, hip-heist back or turn in toward your man to face him.

You are next in a referee's position and the top man has hooked you with the cross-leg ride. You want to *prevent complete arm capture.* If he hooks your far (right) arm, lock your hands in front of your stomach. Next, push into him so that you are sitting on your far hip. Slide your hips away from him and try to get as perpendicular as possible. Post your hooked elbow on the mat so that it anchors you and prevents him from pulling it toward him as much as he wants. Once your elbow is positioned, extend it away from your side, upward, to 45 degrees, to 90, to 120, and so on. You will strain his arm and usually he will pull it out. If he doesn't, although he may suffer from the pressure, you continue to extend, perhaps to 150 degrees. As you move from 120 to 150, pull your chest and bring your elbow in front perpendicular with your chest. He will unhook himself when the pain becomes too intense. Once you free your arm, slide your hips away and raise your back into a sitting position. Keep the near arm and elbow pointed. Wedge your forearm between his body and yours and push away. Be prepared for him to come across your head and take you toward your back. Tuck your chin and pull the palm of your hand into your forehead to establish an incline between forehead and hand and stop him from whipping back your head. Once you see that arm coming, you can be sure he is going after your head. He cannot lean into you now, but he will try to drive in toward you. Post with your free leg and rip the hooked leg out of there. It is hard but possible, and it is a good counter.

Another counter is a *high leg over with underarm control.* This technique is similar to the hip heist, but in this case one leg is posted and the free leg swings high over the posted leg. This changes the elevation of the hip on the high-leg side and turns the body 90 to 180 degrees, depending on the need. Sit again into his near hip. Swing your free leg into a high leg over. Drive your back and head into his chest to pin or stabilize him between your back and the mat. When you have him more or less stabilized, kick another high leg over, using the same leg as before—in this case, your right leg. Lift your hips up off

GENERAL DEFENSIVE POSITIONS

the deck, high leg over, so that you turn toward him. As you step over his hips, you will see that he is on his back and your chest is turned toward the mat. If you do it quickly enough, you will be able to pull out and meet him—chest-to-chest. As you come up, you are now in a Turk ride, a position of significance.

High leg over with overarm control: Once the offensive wrestler has gone over your shoulder, grab his elbow with the arm he is trying to capture. Then he can capture your arm any way he wants to—just make sure you get his elbow. Once you have the elbow, the next step is to sit your hip toward the mat on the near side of the leg that he has hooked. By doing this, you extend him. Keep your near arm tightly to your side. You have knocked him down to his near hip and want next to squirm through. He may trap your head temporarily but without much control. Push your free arm between the bodies. Once your shoulder pops out from under his shoulder, extend and straighten out your near arm across his body. When you have done this, you control him—he must fight to stay off his back. He may release a leg or he may try to stay with it. In most cases, he will at least try to gain a sound base rather than be trapped on his back and lose not only the reversal, but also back points. A good counter, then, against an over-the-shoulder attack is to sit on the near hip and try to work the near arm between his body and yours.

If your opponent has you in a cross ride and breaks you to your far side, do not let him complete a Jacob's arm hook. Control his elbow. Push toward him to force him to push back, a desired reaction. Now drag his arm between your bodies. As you slide your hips away from him, one of two things happens: (1) He may catch you in a Jacob's arm hook. If he does get himself perpendicular with his back up in the air, grab his elbow and purposely drag out very quickly, drawing your hips away and curling your free arm over him and into his rear crotch. (2) If he has not secured a Jacob's arm hook and you drag by, then come up into a cross ride. As you slide your hips away and start to go behind him to prevent him from following, interchange positions by simply rotating the leg. From behind, take his crotch with your free arm and seize his far ankle to stop him from standing. Trap the ankle by shoving his heel up into his buttocks.

Counter to a Turk ride: When you counter a Turk ride, watch for the cradle. From the Turk ride, work the knee of the high leg between your body and your opponent. Be sure the top wrestler does not trap that leg behind your knee—a first step in forming a cradle. And do not let him go around your neck, the second step in securing a cradle.

Once your top leg is between the two bodies, then push away from your opponent. At the same time, turn toward your stomach. Pull your hooked leg in a hip-heisting manner—it is not a true hip—as you turn toward your four-point base.

One final word about countering legs: Technique is important, but so is explosive action.

PINNING DEFENSE

We have known many otherwise exceptional wrestlers who did not know how to get off their backs, mainly because they never practiced from that position. Yet almost every wrestler is put on his back at some point in his career. Therefore, every wrestler should practice and learn how to get off his back. He should have his practice partner make him work out of a half nelson and inside crotch, and out of cradles and back hooks. Because the emphasis in wrestling today is on pinning, it is most important that all wrestlers know how to defend against pins.

Generally, if the man on the bottom tries continuously to set up his offense, keep his head and knees apart, and strive for hand control, the chances are good that he won't get trapped in a pinning combination.

Let's assume however, that you are the down man and are caught in a half nelson and inside crotch. What do you do? First, neck and shoulder bridge from one side to the other. Use your neck to elevate your right shoulder. As you come down, and before going back up into a high bridge, wedge the near arm between your two bodies. Rebridge again, wedge the far arm between both bodies. Each time you come down, turn a little more toward your stomach. Bridge and work your arms between the two bodies, pushing it further and further each time to make it more difficult for the top man to maintain his hold. He loses his angle and his position with each bridge and rotation. Any time you get caught in a nelson, an inside crotch, a body press, or a head lever and a bar, there is no easy escape. You must elevate, work your arm, elevate again, work the arms, and so on. It is hard work, but you have to keep at it until you are free.

Cradles: Cradles neutralize your back and leg power by forcing your knee and head close together. You can discover this yourself easily enough: Place yourself in an upright position. Touch your head to your knees. Have someone hold you this way and try mustering force to escape. It is very hard. Suppose the controlling wrestler has

GENERAL DEFENSIVE POSITIONS

you in a cradle. The first thing you do to escape is work toward your stomach and expand your body. Stretch your arms and neck. Be certain that your knees and legs are as far away from your head as possible. Assume a four-point position. Expand until the controlling wrestler's hands can no longer touch each other. That is your first line of defense against a cradle.

Let us assume the controlling wrestler has broken you to your side. Summon all the force you can. Hook the instep or the toe of your controlled leg with your free leg. Then place either hand, probably the down hand (the one nearest to the mat) on the knee of the controlled leg. Move your other arm on top of that, pull with your free leg, push with both hands, count to 3, and explode. As you do, pull your leg down, push your knee with your hands and try to straighten your back.

Another method of countering cradles is to **recradle.** The top man has a front cradle or a straight cradle and has locked you up. You have a free arm (the near arm is generally pinned between the bodies). Post and brace with that free arm. Elevate your upper body as much as possible. As you post and brace, turn into the cradle of the controlling wrestler. One of two things will happen. Your near arm will pop through. If that is the case, you are in good position beause the controlling wrestler will begin to lose some balance and give you the chance to spread both arms and gain a base. When he sees that he cannot take you either way, but continues to hold onto his cradle, he could find himself in a dangerous position. He might also just release his cradle grip and attack your lower body.

Suppose you have not come off the bottom, but have at least broken the cradle. The next step as you turn in toward the controlling man is to force your near arm around his neck. As you do this, brace your far arm and slide your hips away from him. While you slide, tighten up your near arm around his neck. Bring the braced arm in behind the knee of his near leg. Place your inside leg between his legs to block the lower far leg from stepping over, and continue to slide your hips out further. Both of you are lying on your sides. Whoever gets height more quickly is going to be most successful in recradling.

If the down wrestler has recradled or achieved his own cradle, the next step is to break the cradle altogether by expanding the outside leg and posting it. With hip-heisting force, lift your opponent's far leg—backward as hard as you can. Because of the precarious position your opponent is now in, he usually will release his cradle and try to secure himself before disaster occurs.

Expansions and recradling are the basic methods for getting out of a cradle. Many coaches will tell you that if you do not want to get pinned in a cradle, do not get caught in one. It is not that simple.

Back hooks: A back hook occurs when the top wrestler catches the arm of the bottom wrestler at the elbow on the bicep side and pulls the bottom wrestler toward his back. Whenever your opponent has you in a back hook and begins to pull your elbow to your hip, turn the palm of your hand toward his forehead. As he pulls, he pulls your palm into his forehead. When you reach his forehead, your arm will be extended and ready to post. Push with that arm and straighten your body too. That expansion and stretching will break his back hook because his hand will then slide from your elbow up to your shoulder. Your shoulder should be stronger than his hook and if you turn toward him, you should free yourself from the back hook.

5

Becoming a Good Wrestler

To become a good wrestler requires unbending commitment. It is always easier not to become one. To truly commit yourself to wrestling, you must honor the sport and give it the necessary time, energy, and intelligence. An intelligent wrestler is one who has learned how to wrestle within his limitations. Every wrestler has certain strengths and weaknesses that influence the way he plans his attack. He must know his best moves and work with those to make them more effective. When he gambles on unfamiliar or unrehearsed tactics, he risks defeat.

Learn to wrestle under pressure and learn how to use momentum. When you feel the match has shifted your way, open up your offense a little. Try different moves, shoot more often. Take advantage, keep the pressure on, keep charging, keep your opponent guessing and worried. There are moments, of course, when your opponent stops your momentum or turns it to his advantage. Then you have to regain it.

In football, if the quarterback has a bad day, his coach takes him out of the game. Once a wrestler moves onto the mat, he has to go all the way, regardless of how he feels or the kind of day he is having. You must realize that you are not going to be as sharp in some matches as others. However, if you know that you are in good condition, have good technique, and have confidence in yourself, then you can persevere on those off days. You may have to vary your attack and employ other maneuvers or, in other words, compensate for your lack of sharpness in that particular match, but that is where your intelligence as a wrestler comes in. Never lose confidence. Thinking, feeling, and anticipating and desiring victory must always be preeminent in your mind.

Make your opponent lose. Sometimes your opponent will give up 30 seconds after the bout has started, or he won't surrender until the last 10 seconds, or, sometimes, never. You must never give up, regardless of the score, the period, the time, the situation. Think always of winning.

There will be times during a bout when something shakes your confidence. You may find yourself in a situation you were not prepared for or accustomed to. This happens all the time—it is a part of wrestling, although good wrestlers work extra hard to minimize the unexpected.

Sometimes adverse situations occur when a wrestler's concentration temporarily fails him. This can occur as a result of fatigue, overconfidence, lack of confidence, whatever. A good wrestler seldom has a problem with concentration. He is always thinking ahead. If you have practiced anticipating problems and responses to those problems, you will not lose your concentration or panic on the mat. For this reason, it is important to practice real bout situations.

SETTING GOALS

In the course of the season, set goals for yourself. As you progress through the season, your mistakes should diminish, improvements should increase, conditioning should get better—everything should improve if you have set the right goals and are working with the right degree of effort.

You should evaluate your goals at different points throughout the season and compare your rate of progress to those goals.

The idea of goal orientation is vital for us at Princeton, but we try to be sure that our wrestlers and we as coaches aim for the "right" ones. An undefeated goal is not necessarily the right goal. A deep commitment toward self-improvement is more important to us in the long run because it insures concentration on the right values, the idea of improvement of athletic skills. Winning follows hard work and improvement and should not be an end in itself. We always try, for example, to defeat our opponent as badly as possible, not because we like to inflict suffering or humiliation but because our wrestlers seek constantly to improve their level of skill.

Because of the nature of college wrestling, our season is actually three miniature seasons—one is prior to Christmas, the second is in the dead of winter, and the third is the tournament season. For each of those mini-seasons, we reevaluate our goals and ask ourselves tough questions: Are our goals realistic? Are we exceeding them? Have we set them too low? Are we working hard enough? We can then adjust our thinking, our practices, and we hope, if necessary, our performance, according to the answers we find for these questions.

Any discussion about what it takes to become an outstanding wrestler must always return to a single truth: There is no single factor involved. Certainly attitude and physical attributes count substantially. Weak wrestlers cannot win. Strong wrestlers who are not in good physical shape cannot succeed. Strong, well-conditioned, highly skilled wrestlers who lack the will to win cannot win. The outstanding wrestler has a capacity for hard work and a determination to improve that quickly separates him from the ordinary wrestler.

PRACTICE

There is only one way to improve and that is to practice, practice, practice. There is no easy way or shortcut. It is all hard work. The real measure of success is not what you can do in comparison to others, but what you do relative to your own potential. Development of any skill is based on three fundamentals: The first is to learn from a master teacher; the second is to love wrestling; and the third is to work extra hard.

Learn a particular maneuver, then practice it to make it perfect. Once you know it, you are ready to learn another one, but know one move well first, especially how to execute the maneuver from both right and left sides. It is good to practice four or five maneuvers in each position—neutral, bottom, top. Use them in different situations and employ new approaches to the execution of the moves.

Practice the right skills. Necessity is the mother of invention. If you are short, develop moves that fit your physique. If you are tall, take advantage of your height.

If you are ever in doubt about the mechanics of any particular technique, consult your coach, check the opinions of others, test your problem under combative drill at practice, and analyze the results.

SKILL DEVELOPMENT

Every practice at Princeton can be divided into two categories: skill development and conditioning. (See chapter 6 for a list of skill improvement drills.) Skill development begins with the basics: stance, motion, penetration—one move built upon another starting with the drop step down to the mat. Each practice will stress some particular aspect or combination of the neutral, top, and bottom positions.

At our level we try to expose every wrestler to as much wrestling as time, schedule, and competition permit. Some coaches try to teach their wrestlers to do the same maneuvers the same way. Others teach a particular maneuver but let the individual pick out aspects of the move that best fit his wrestling style. Not everybody has the same ability to master specific skills, so it is important for coaches to have a basic philosophy but not insist on uniformity to the exclusion of individuality.

Our basic rule is that every wrestler must be able to take down his opponent. The wrestlers have an opportunity to select those moves that best suit their body structure and their talent. Our basic guideline for a down wrestler is that he be able to get off the bottom quickly. We don't try to change a wrestler's specific style, unless, of course, he is unsuccessful. Then we go back to basics. Only in a situation where a wrestler does not experience success do we try to change his style.

Many coaches teach their kids to win 3-2,2-1,4-3. Others try to teach a wide variety of skills. In high-school wrestling today, too many coaches teach their kids only to win. They wrestle two times a week and prepare for the match two days a week, easing off, brushing up on some drills, but not doing much heavy work and not receiving much instruction. Perhaps they have one good day of teaching a week or, at most, two days. There should be more teaching time in the lower levels of competition. The junior-high wrestler should master a limited number of techniques. The more teaching days, and the more skill-development days a coach can incorporate into his program, the higher the degree of learning will be.

In our early season practices, we spend a considerable amount of time in skill development—less time by comparison in conditioning. As we go through the season, we spend less time in skill teaching and more on conditioning. The length of practices becomes shorter since there is less instruction.

DAILY PRACTICE SCHEDULE

Our practices, usually in the late afternoon at Princeton, last 1½ hours. We work on three areas. The first is warm-up. We go through a set routine each day:

First, a basic drill, the drop-step drill, that signals the beginning of practice and gets everyone into the right frame of mind.

Then we go to "favorites": takedowns, reversals, escapes, breakdowns, and pins. This is a time for each wrestler to express his individuality. This period helps us develop a "feel" for who our athletes are and what they are doing. They work on their specialities. They perfect or brush up or add to their skills. This period serves also as warm-up and gets us into our practice with an efficient expenditure of time.

The next part is skill development or drills—a major part of practice in the early season. It is almost a clinic because we teach everything we would like our wrestlers to be exposed to that year. It lasts about 3 weeks. This is where we play by our rules. Not every wrestler, for example, likes a duck under, but we make everybody go through a duck under so that he has a working knowledge of it. Some may learn to like it.

We teach through demonstration and we incorporate wrestlers into the process, asking them to explain techniques—in effect, to help us teach. They have a chance to express themselves in front of the team and to show what they know and can do well. It also makes them stop and analyze how they perform specific moves so it makes them better at that particular skill.

We work slowly at first. Whenever we try to develop a skill we first lay a solid foundation by going through the drill in a slow, deliberate style. For drills that use several body movements, we number each movement in a progression. Once the proper movements are acquired then we increase the speed and the power, but only after the slow, methodical steps are mastered. Once the foundation is built, then we emphasize speed and power.

As the year picks up, the pace must accelerate, especially toward tournament time when the emphasis by then should be on execution, speed, power, and stamina.

We simulate and exaggerate bout conditions. In college we use a 2-3-3 bout, but in practices we will sometimes go 2-3-3-1 or 5-5-5. Sometimes we will shorten the duration and go 1-1-1 and work what we call mini-bouts and do two or three of them in succession. We will simulate bout situations. We like to do regulation bouts and finish with 1 minute on our feet. How often near the end of the bout do wrestlers find themselves on their feet? If they are not schooled in shooting takedowns when they are tired, they are at a disadvantage.

A major reason for exaggerating bout conditions is to increase the stress on our wrestlers. A real bout has peaks and valleys of activity, explosions, periods of rest, more explosions, and so on. In our third phase of practice, the combative phase, we simulate these conditions, pressing our wrestlers toward exhaustion, then slacking off to allow them to recuperate, going strong again, and so on, all the while trying to increase their ability to withstand stress. Another name for this type of work is *interval training*. We go through 10 to 12 minutes of hard combat, then give them a 2 to 3-minute break before we resume. As the year goes on, it takes less time during these breaks for the wrestlers to recover, a sign of improving endurance.

A WEEKLY PRACTICE SCHEDULE

Monday: We usually discuss the results of the previous meet (most of our meets are on weekends) and what we expect to encounter in the next meet. We then follow a regular practice routine, including warm-up, drop-step drill, the favorites, and so on. Drills are a major part of Monday's practice, especially in those areas where we were weak in the previous meet. Then we drill for our upcoming opponents. In the third part of practice, the combatives, we usually go one or two bouts. We interject whistle starts, situation scrimmages, variations of bouts, 5-5-5's or 2-3-3's with a 1-minute period on the feet at the end, and mini-bouts, perhaps three in succession, changing partners after each bout for variety of countering ability and body type. We save 2 to 5 minutes for the captain at the end of the practice. On different days he will have them do different things, such as some sort of circuit training drill that has a lot of wrestling techniques in it, some sprints, or a little distance running. It is a conditioning period, and it also gives the captain an opportunity to demonstrate his leadership ability.

Tuesday, Wednesday, and Thursday: Basically, we do the same thing in the first part of practice, but in the second part we may spend more time on takedowns.

On Wednesday and Thursday we devote time to the down position. As we work toward Saturday, the day of the match, the combative drills become the prime focus of the practice.

Friday: We call Friday our "weight-making day," but we do not force wrestlers to make specific weights. Most wrestlers know how much weight they can lose. We advise our wrestlers if they consult us, but they themselves generally decide at what weight they want to wrestle. A program is in deep trouble if the wrestlers have to worry more about losing weight than developing their own skills.

Friday is really a day for psychological and physical preparation for the match. Each wrestler prepares differently. As coaches, we have prepared them for the physical aspect. It is now up to them to be ready for the mental part. We do require that everyone show up at practice on Friday at a specified time and that everyone break a sweat in the room. Once they have done that, they are free to do as they wish.

As we go through a season, our practice time decreases from about an hour and a half to just a little over an hour. We organize our practices so that no one is left standing around waiting for mat space or for partners. We also suggest that coaches be in the practice room an hour before practice starts and after practice, too, for individual help.

CONDITIONING

We consider every practice in its entirety to be a conditioning session, but, of course, we also recognize that the furious all-out pace of a real bout, when the wrestler may use every muscle in his body for a prolonged period of time (or so it seems to him), requires long, hard physical training.

It takes approximately 1 week of vigorous training to prepare for each minute of a wrestling bout. The first 4 weeks of practice should be devoted to running, rope climbing, exercising, handball, paddle ball, and light work on wrestling drills.

As time passes and your body becomes conditioned to the skills you want to master, spend less time on exercising and more on drills and competitive bouts. Running and rope climbing continue to be useful exercises throughout the season, but they should be done after the drill work. We want our wrestlers to be fresh during the learning and drill sessions, not fatigued and susceptible to bad habits.

Some coaches worry about their wrestlers going "stale," a physical condition whose symptoms are constant listlessness and tiredness. Though infrequently, this does occur in most good athletes. We would rather see a boy become stale than never reach optimum condition. A wrestler should never overprotect himself but should punish his body to improve his effectiveness.

Developing endurance is only one aspect of conditioning. Another is development of strength. Our wrestlers improve their strength primarily through weight training. They may use any one of three basic weight-training methods: conventional weights, such as barbells and dumbbells; a Universal gym; or a Nautilus machine. Whichever approach you take, develop a simple program and stick with it. Lift weights throughout the year, because increase in strength takes a long time.

6

Skill Improvement Drills

For wrestlers to react quickly and correctly in combat, they must have the chance to practice realistic drills daily. We will discuss skill improvement drills in four areas: *neutral, bottom position, top position,* and *general mat drills.*

NEUTRAL POSITION

Drop-step drill: We described this fundamental drill in chapter 1. It can be done with or without a partner.

Hand combat: Both wrestlers spar with each other trying to control one another's hands and arms. From referee's position, each wrestler hits the other on chest with palm of hand, arm not fully extended. One wrestler tries tie-up: collar and bicep, collar and tricep, double bicep, double tricep, wrist and collar, double wrist. At same time, other wrestler tries to ward off, maintaining good defensive position. Do not try to complete moves in this drill.

Leg offense/defense drill: One wrestler is on defense—takes a good stance, a bit more erect than normal. Hands on either hip, or arms straight out parallel to the ground. Second wrestler is on offense—takes sound neutral attacking position. On command, offensive man penetrates for double leg. At same time, defensive wrestler tries to defend from double leg. Defensive wrestler sprawls, goes to quarter nelson or cross face or head drive—into any quick move that will ward off the attacker. Defensive wrestler's prime responsibility is to sprawl and defend properly.

Football tackling dummy: Use a regular blocking dummy, about 4 feet high. Hit dummy and see how far you can drive it, as if penetrating an opponent. Drive dummy and lift it.

90-second shooting drill: Offensive man goes all out—set-up, shoot, takedown. Defensive man wards off, but cannot retreat. He can move laterally or forward, but not backward. Switch positions after 90 seconds.

Set-up—contact, non contact: Practice full-speed set-ups of both kinds followed by shot at opponent's legs.

15-second defense drill: Offensive wrestler attacks all out for 15 seconds. Drill simulates desperation offense late in bout.

Upper body drill: Practice takedown from waist up only.

Pancake and counter: Offensive wrestler shoots double leg. Defender stops forward penetration and counters with pancake. Do right or left.

Shoot, defend, shoot: One wrestler shoots. Defender retaliates with counter. Do in rapid succession.

BOTTOM

Hip-heist drill: Sit on buttocks. Bring heels up in comfortable position so that knees are bent at greater than 90-degree angle. Place hands alongside hips, a couple of inches behind. Lift hips in air. Pressure is now on four points, feet and hands. Now, rotate body in 180-degree turn. Post right leg and left hand, lift right hip in air, and move left hip and leg underneath right. Balance on your hand, right hand comes up in air. From back position, go toward front. You are on all fours with stomach toward mat. Repeat it same way in clockwise direction. Post with left leg and right hand, turn right hip underneath left. Brace with right hand to keep hip in air and windmill with left hand so that you end up in the position you originally started in.

High leg over: Post down leg and carry hip and opposite leg over top of down leg. Turn body accordingly.

Shoulder rolls: Two parts. Part I is a rolling drill. Drop down as if going into referee's position. Knees shoulder-width apart, toes

SKILL IMPROVEMENT DRILLS

cocked, hands on hips. Start clockwise. Tuck chin into chest. If you dropped left shoulder to mat, move left shoulder across as if you were a turtle and could tuck in your head. Carry knees over your head. Do not carry knees over chest. Too many wrestlers do that and fall on their backs. Your cocked toes push and elevate hips over and the hips carry the knees over your head. The hip-knee action transfers weight from left shoulder to right (or vice versa). Continue in one direction about 6 times, then stop; put other shoulder down, reverse directions, and repeat.

Part II is done from a sitting position. Pull heels up under buttocks. Hook hands right under thighs in bend of your knees. As heels come back to hips, hands tighten up. Tuck chin into chest. Moving clockwise, drop to your left side. Dig your left toe into the mat and lift your hips into the air. Push across the top of your shoulders onto your right side and come up in a sitting position. You have gone from left side 360 degrees to the right side. Do this drill in reverse.

Stand-up: Assume referee's position. Opponent lines up on your left side. On command, move left foot directly underneath your head, straighten your head, and bring left arm across your head, in front of your face, lifting and pointed up in the air. Watch your index finger and get your head up to follow through. This uplifting brings your trailing leg under your hip and helps elevate your upper body.

Inside leg stand-up: Place a sandbag on your back. Stand up and move left leg across, underneath head and reach up in air with hand. If you do not move that trailing leg quickly enough, sandbag will roll off your back and fall on calf of down leg.

Belly-up: Bottom man is prone. Top man can use any hold he wishes. Bottom man will now try to get to good base. He rotates to one side, brings high leg knee up under chest and rolls back to high side, over the high leg, and brings both knees up under chest. This drill helps wrestlers learn how to get to a base position.

Fight off cradle: For spurts of 10 to 15 seconds, one wrestler assumes cradle position with opponent holding knees and head. He then tries to break cradle.

Limp arm: Bottom man often has arm tied up, usually from tight-laced near-arm situation. Bottom wrestler slaps top man's belly and, as he does, tries to withdraw his arm from bar hold of top wrestler. He allows top man to bar the arm again, then limp arm's out: bar, limp arm, bar, limp arm, repeating 5 to 10 times each side; then switch and let the other man work the bar and tight waist from the top.

TOP

Ankle checks: On whistle command, top man checks for far ankle, catches it at instep, forcefully drives heel into buttocks and turns foot across buttocks to exert pressure. Emphasize speed.

Breakdowns off whistle start: Purpose is to condition wrestler's motion off the whistle. Can practice any breakdown he wants.

Defensive base—10 seconds: Bottom man tries to keep good base. Top man in turn tries to destroy that base. Switch positions after 10 seconds.

MAT DRILLS

Spinning: Bottom man assumes referee's position. Top man places chest on bottom man, as if their bodies were connected by axis through chest. Rotate around bottom man; use hands to sense position of bottom man. Move legs accordion style, 360 degrees. The beginning wrestler will require 5 or 6 steps to complete a circle; the veteran wrestler may be able to do it in one step. Spin in both directions.

There are two offshoots of the spinning drill: (1) bottom man collapses right or left shoulder as signal to top man to change direction; (2) bottom wrestler extends one of his arms to block, again causing top man to change direction.

Floating: Bottom man changes from one position to another to set up various holds but he is not allowed to lock grip or hook in this drill. The top man checks himself into a position of safety with each change of position by the bottom man. The purpose is not to control the bottom man but to get to safe position to meet each change by the bottom man.

20-second switch drill: Bottom man practices switch at varying speeds and from both right and left. Progression should be from slow (emphasizing technique) to fast (emphasizing speed). Do at intervals of 20 seconds. Length of time and speed depends on skill level of wrestlers.

Leg drill: This drill will help young wrestlers learn how to react to legs. Down wrestler takes referee's position; top wrestler interlocks leg in cross ride. Down man sits either to near hip or to far hip and top man has to react. In other words, down man tries to counter cross ride and top man must react to counter attempt.

Hand control: 15 to 20 seconds. Both wrestlers vie for hand control, blocking and covering, trying to escape or reverse opponent.

Switch, reswitch: Defensive wrestler initiates a switch. Offensive wrestler counters and reswitches. Each wrestler will switch and reswitch for 10 to 15 seconds.

7

Weight-Training Exercises

Here are some general rules about weightlifting and the exercise we use for dumbbells and for the Universal.

It is essential that you warm up properly to avoid muscle strain with a set or two of light weight exercises. Simple calisthenics are not sufficient.

Proper breathing is important only for exercises that expand the chest cavity (bench, leg, and shoulder presses; lateral pulls). The correct procedure for breathing is to "blow the weight up"—exhale as you pull or press the weight up.

CONVENTIONAL WEIGHT-TRAINING EXERCISES

We perform each of the following exercises 3 times with a total of 10 repetitions each time, lifting approximately 80 percent of the weight-lifter's maximum capacity.

Two-arm wrist curl: Sit down with your forearms on thighs. Wrists on knees, hold bar, palms up. Raise bar from resting position. Flex and extend. Do 10 times for 3 sets. Amount of weight should be approximately 80 percent of what you can potentially lift. Challenge yourself in last few repetitions of each set.

Two-arm curl: Stand with hands shoulder width apart. Flex arms, bring bar to neck or top of chest, then return.

Two-arm reverse curl: Grab bar with palms down; raise bar to chest; return to resting position.

Military press: Arms, shoulder-width apart. Raise bar to chest, press over your head.

WEIGHT-TRAINING EXERCISES

Bench press: Lie down with bar over chest, then push it directly over arms to full extension before lowering.

Upright roll: Stand, hold bar 2 to 3 inches apart; raise bar along chest to neck level; then return to full arm extension.

Bent rolling: Bend over in L position, legs spread apart. Raise bar to chest, then return to full extension.

Dead lift: Feet shoulder width apart. Lean over, grab bar with palms facing back toward legs; straighten body to full upright position; return bar to floor.

Toe raises: Place weight behind head, resting on shoulders. Hold weight with hands shoulder width apart. Feet approximately shoulder width apart, heels resting on floor, toes on 2-inch board or 2-inch incline. Raise to full extension of foot, upward direction; then relax, setting back until heels rest on floor.

Half squat: Put weight over shoulders behind head, feet approximately shoulder width apart. Dip down to half squat, hold for a second, then return to full upright position.

An optional eleventh exercise: Do 3 sets of 20 sit-ups on incline board, increasing number of repetitions as you get stronger.

UNIVERSAL WEIGHT PROGRAM

We have borrowed these drills from Pennsbury High School in Fairless Hills, Pennsylvania.

Chest press: Lie flat on bench with legs bent and feet on floor. Grasp bar with hands more than shoulder width apart. Raise weight straight up then lower to chest.

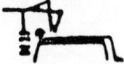

Leg press: Sit erect in chair. Use peddle where range of motion is shorter to prevent hyperextension of ligaments. Do not let weight come back to position until you finish lift.

Shoulder press: Use high stool to prevent leg use. Get directly under bar to maintain 90-degree angle. Press bar over head until elbows are fully extended. Lower bar to chest.

Pulley chains: Kneel under bar. Pull to chest. Do not let legs leave floor when returning bar to position.

Leg curls: Lie flat on leg bench face down. Place both heels under padded leg bar. Raise legs to 90 degrees and let weight down slowly.

Arm curls: Feet 10 to 12 inches apart. Flex elbows fully. Lift bar upward toward chest. Keep elbows close to sides and avoid raising shoulders. Do not lean backward or bounce bar with leg motion.

Dipping: Pull through range of motion. Try to touch armpits to bar on every repetition.

Sit-ups: Lie with back on bench, knees bent. Put arms behind head. Sit up until elbows touch knees. When sit-up becomes easier, change incline of board.

Chinning: Use straight-up-and-down motion with no swinging. Go through full range of motion.

Tri-extension: Stand straight up starting with bar at shoulders. Pull weight down to waist keeping elbows in—no back movement.

Neck exercise: Put head in head harness. Put hands on waist and stand up. Pull weight just with neck, not back. Pull weight to front, back, side.

Posture row: Using curl bar, step away from machine, bend knees. With arms extended, pull weight to chest; do not use back, use only arms, shoulders.

Appendix: Instructions for a Match

Use common sense after weighing in, especially if you have had to diet. Do not load up on junk food prior to a meet; it will give you no nutritional substance.

Before the match, eat and drink those items that give quick energy—hot beef bouillon, hot tea, honey, dextrose. They are satisfying as well as nutritious. Cold drinks are not recommended. Remember, dieting over the weekend, after a match, is just as important as before.

During the match, encourage each team member to do as well as he can. Do not let anyone think his points are not important in the final score.

While awaiting your match, watch other wrestlers for methods of attack, strategies, maneuvers, and styles. Always try to learn.

Warm up carefully and thoroughly before entering a match.

A handshake before and after the bout is sportsmanship enough—hugging, backslapping, and so on are superfluous.

When returning to the center of the mat, always walk back to your position, take deep breaths, decide your next series of maneuvers, relax and loosen up a bit, and keep loose and ready to explode.

Remember the main objective in wrestling throughout the match: the fall.

Be in condition to wear down all opponents, trying for a pin especially in the latter part of the bout.

Stay at right angles in pinning combinations.

Always stay on balance and keep your opponent off balance.

Be aggressive and carry the battle to your opponent. Feint him into wrestling your style; wrestle first to win, then to pin; know the value of being in the position of advantage.

Never forget your own position and safety at any second.

Use maneuvers in a logical sequence.

Never relax for one instant when in contact with your opponent. If necessary, it should be done only when you are out of range and have a safe but alert defense.

Be versatile in all phases of wrestling—takedowns, reversals, rides, etc.

Vary your attack.

Always be one step ahead of your opponent—this comes through hard practice and conditioning.

When wrestling from the *neutral position:*
- Don't muscle.
- Develop effective feints.
- Work man into best position for takedowns.
- Work opponent's deficiencies into position that you can capitalize on with your best moves.
- When you attack, attack with full power and do not stop driving until you either have takedown or there is no more contact.
- Never, under any circumstance, backpedal.
- Always be alert for unexpected.

When wrestling from the *offensive position:*
- Master effective breakdowns.
- Keep your opponent tied up.
- Make him carry your weight.
- Keep good body contact.
- Be cautious of your position on the mat proper.
- Wear him down before pinning.
- When beginning a match anew, change over from side to side, always your best side first.
- Keep man flat on the deck.
- Give 1-point escape rather than 2-point reversal.

When wrestling from the *defensive position:*
- Do not lose your base position.
- Never let arm or arms get behind you.
- Never get flattened on stomach.
- Keep head off mat.
- Keep in a ball position.
- Explode on all attempted escapes and reversals.
- Move in series until you have scored.
- When in doubt, stand.

Glossary

Advantage. Same as Control.

Advantage time. Same as Riding time.

Ankle attack. A maneuver aimed at lifting the opponent's ankle off the mat, as a means to secure or improve control.

Ankle ride. Top man controls his opponent by holding his ankle and doubling his leg back.

Arm bar. Top man holds the forearm of his opponent and presses with the upper part of his other arm against the back of his opponent's elbow or upper arm.

Arm drags. Maneuvers by which a wrestler grabs his opponent's arm and pulls or posts it in order to go behind.

Bottom position. When a wrestler assumes a four-point stance at the start of a period or when a referee signals a restart, he is in the bottom position, the position of disadvantage.

Bow and arrow cradle. Leverage hold. Opponent uses his head as a fulcrum and pulls on his opponent's neck and leg, bending him like a bow.

Break down. Maneuver intended to knock out the opponent's supporting points and flatten him to the mat.

Bridge. A move in which the opponent about to be pinned braces his body on top of head, elbows, and feet to keep shoulders off the mat.

Control One wrestler is positioned in such a way (behind and above his opponent) that his opponent is immobilized or restrained.

Counter. A maneuver in which one wrestler stops or reverses a maneuver by his opponent, to his advantage.

Cradle. A pinning maneuver in which one wrestler holds his opponent's head and leg in his arms and forces them toward each other, locking his hands.

Cross body. One wrestler drives his body across his opponent's body by hooking one of his opponent's legs with his own.

Cross face. One wrestler drives his forearm across his opponent's face and lifts his head by gripping his shoulder with his driving hand.

Defensive position. Same as bottom position.

Double armlock. One wrestler locks his arm around his opponent's body from the front after reaching through his arms.

Double grapevine. One wrestler on top of his opponent interlocks his legs around his opponent's legs to prevent him from rolling.

Double-leg takedown. One wrestler attacks his opponent's legs in an effort to take him to the mat.

Duck under. Maneuver in which one wrestler slips his head under his opponent's arm and uses his head as a fulcrum for leverage.

Escape. One wrestler frees himself from the control of the other.

Fall. A wrestler holds his man's shoulders or area of both scapulas to the mat for 1 second (in college) 2 seconds (in high school).

Far-arm hook. From the top position, a wrestler reaches over his opponent's body and hooks his supporting arm in the crook of his arm.

Finish-off. The final step in an offensive move that completes control of the opponent.

Fishhook. Forming the hand into a fishhooklike shape to stop momentum and redirect force of the opponent.

Forward roll. An escape or reverse in which one wrestler puts his shoulders to the mat and rolls rapidly and forcefully across them.

Full nelson. One opponent applies pressure against the back of his opponent's neck by reaching under his arms and locking his hands behind his neck. An illegal and dangerous hold.

Grapevine. A wrestler entwines one of his legs around one of his opponent's legs, gripping with his instep against his shin.

Guillotine. A pinning hold combination in which a wrestler employs a cross-leg ride on one leg and a head lever under one of his opponent's arms and around his neck.

GLOSSARY

Half nelson. One wrestler reaches under his opponent's arm from the rear and uses the back of his opponent's head or neck for leverage.

Hammerlock. One wrestler grips his opponent's arm, uses his back as a fulcrum, and pries with his forearm.

Head lever. One wrestler raises his opponent's arm by gripping his wrist and lifts and drives his head under his opponent's arm.

Heel pick. One wrestler drops low, grips his opponent by the back of the heel and pulls the leg up toward him.

Inside crotch hold. One wrestler reaches between his opponent's legs and uses his forearm as a lever to prevent him from turning.

Jacob's hook. An arm entwinement forcing the immobilization of the defensive wrestler's arm.

Mat. The soft padded material used as the wrestling arena.

Match. A competition between two wrestlers.

Near fall. A position in which the offensive wrestler has his opponent in a controlled pinning situation.

Nelson. A series of wrestling holds that features leverage applied under the armpit and behind the neck.

Neutral position. Both wrestlers face each other on their feet or on their knees with neither man in control.

Offensive position. Same as top position.

One-on-one. The offensive wrestler uses one hand to control one hand of the defensive wrestler.

Pancake. One wrestler ensnares his opponent's arm with his arm and drives his opponent backward over his base with the free arm.

Penalty points. Points awarded to one wrestler when his opponent violates a rule or procedure.

Penetration. One wrestler drives deep through his opponent's defenses.

Pin. See Fall.

Referee's position. Starting position for the opening of the second and third periods of a match and for all restarts not from a neutral position. Wrestlers take a top and bottom as directed by the referee.

Reswitch. One wrestler allows himself to switch with his opponent and depends on the force of his momentum to regain his original top position.

Reversal. A 2-point scoring move that occurs when one wrestler frees himself of the control of his opponent and gains control.

Reverse nelson. One wrestler lifts against the back of his opponent's head by reaching under his arm from in front of him.

Riding time. The net amount of time one wrestler controls his opponent.

Roll. A series of maneuvers in which one wrestler rolls his opponent's weight, placing himself momentarily on his side and back or across his shoulders.

Scissors. One wrestler encircles his opponent's thigh with his legs and squeezes him by crossing his ankles.

Set-up. A maneuver by which one wrestler tries to gain a slight advantage by feinting, pulling, pushing, or making noises to distract his opponent.

Single-leg takedown. Any maneuver by which an attacking wrestler gains control of one of his opponent's legs to force him to the mat.

Sit-out. Maneuvers from the bottom by which one wrestler thrusts his feet out to a sitting position on the mat to brace himself and gain a base.

Snapback. A counter to a sit-out in which one wrestler catches his opponent's upper arms in his hands and, with his chin at his shoulder, drops him backward to the mat.

Sprawl. To avoid being caught by the legs by an attacking wrestler, the defensive wrestler drives his hips down onto his opponent's shoulders and thrusts his legs out quickly behind him to break the grip of the attacker.

Stack. A pinning maneuver in which one wrestler lifts his opponent's hips and buttocks above his upper body.

Stalemate. A position other than a pinning situation in which neither wrestler can nor will improve his position.

GLOSSARY

Stalling. Failure to wrestler aggressively. Avoiding action.

Stand-up. A maneuver by which a wrestler on the bottom bursts to his feet.

Takedown. One wrestler takes his opponent to the mat from a neutral position.

Three-quarter nelson. One wrestler applies pressure to the back of his opponent's head or neck with two hands interlocked by reaching under only one arm and under the chest to the far side.

Throw. One wrestler knocks his opponent off his feet and aims his back toward the mat.

Throw-by. The offensive wrestler redirects the direction of the defensive wrestler by use of the existing movement of both wrestlers.

Top position. One wrestler is above and behind his opponent with one arm encircling his waist and another placed loosely on his elbow. Position of advantage.

Tripod. A position in which a bottom wrestler has established a base using two heels and buttocks or two feet and the hand or hands as one post.

Turk ride. The offensive wrestler steps between the legs of the down wrestler and traps him on his side or back.

Two-on-one hold. One wrestler grabs his opponent's arm or wrist with both hands.

Wing roll. A maneuver from the bottom in which one wrestler uses his opponent's momentum catching his arm, pulling down, and elevating his opponent at the same time.

Wrestler's grip. The interlocking of the two hands in order to apply the greatest pressure or lock possible.

Index

Adjustment, 125
Ankle checks, 94–95, 160
   counters to, 140–141
Ankle lift, 134
Arm capture, preventing, 144
Arm curls, 164
Arm drags, 26–28

Back cradle, 104–107
Backheel counter, 134
Back hooks, for pinning defense, 148
Bar arm and hook series, 114–118
Bar arm and Jacob's ride, 120
Barrel roll, 47–48, 58
Barrel-roll tie, 132
Base positions, offensive (from the bottom), 62–64
Bear hug, 42
Belly-up, 159
Bench press, 163
Bent rolling, 163
Body lift, 136–137
Bottom offense, defensing, 132–140
Bottom (skill improvement) drills, 158–159
Bow and arrow cradle, 112

Breakdowns off whistle start, 160
Bridge over cradle, 108–110
Bridge roll, 82–90
   cutting off, 139
Bulldog ride, 95–96
   countering, 141
Butt drive, 134

Chest press, 163
Chinning, 164
Circle drag, 28
Commitment, importance of, 149–150
Conditioning, 154–155
   staleness, 155–156
Contact set-up, 9
Control, 91–92
   and pinning (using the legs), 118–123
Cradles, 104–114
   for pinning defense, 146–148
Cross-body ride, 119–120
Cross duck under, 25
Cross elbow and knee snatch, 31
Cross face, 123
Cross-face cradle, 112–114
Cross-face opposite arm, 131

INDEX 173

Cross wrist control or cross control, 139
Crotch lift, 136
Crunch, 50

Dead lift, 163
Defensive base, 160
Defensive positions, 124–148
   bottom offense, 132–140
   countering upper body attacks, 131–132
   lines of, 124
   neutral position attacks, 125–131
   pinning, 146–148
   top offense, 140–146
Dipping, 164
Double arm bar series, 117–118
Double-leg lift, 137
Double-leg takedown, 14–17
Double trouble, 143
Drop-low and far-ankle drive, 142
Drop-step drill, 11–12, 14, 157
Duck under, 20
Dump, 50

Elbow control, 131
Elbow hook, 131
Endurance, developing, 156
Escapes (offensive moves from the bottom, 64–78
   hip heist, 69
   hip-heist switch, 73–74
   inside leg stand-up, 64–67
   long sit-out, 68
   outside leg stand-up, 67
   outside tripod, 69–70
   overhooks, 76
   scoot away, 72
   short sit series, 68–69
   sit-out and head check, 78
   sit and push back, 69

Exercises. *See* Weight-training exercises
Expansion, 126

Far side cradle, 111
Fifteen-second defense drill, 158
Fight off cradle, 159
Finish-off, 14
Fireman's carry, 48
Floating, 160
Football tackling dummy, 158
Front pressure trip, 22–23

Goals, setting, 150–151
Guillotine, 121–123

Half squat, 163
Hammerlock, 103–104
Hand combat, 157
Hand control, 161
   from the bottom, 139
Head drag, 128
Head drive, 130
Head grab and check, 138–139
Head lever, 98–99
Head spear to knee snatch, 32–33
Heel pick, 42
High-crotch takedown, 34–37
High leg over, 128, 158
   with overarm control, 145
   with underarm control, 144–145
Hip heist, 69
Hip-heist drill, 158
Hip-heist switch, 73–74, 140
Hook series. *See* Bar arm and hook series
Hooks, 118

Inside crotch pry and near-arm chop, 94
Inside leg stand-up, 64–67, 159
Inside sit-out, 144
Interval training, 154

Jacob's hook, 120
Jacob's ride, 120

Knee elevator and trip, 134
Knee lock and extension, 143–144
Kneeling-facing, 61

Lace ride. See Navy ride
Leg curls, 164
Leg drill, 160–161
Leg extension, 143
Leg face and cross pressure, 134–136
Leg offense/defense drill, 157–158
Leg press, 163
Leg pressure, 134
Leg split cradle, 108
Legs off the bottom, countering, 143–146
Legs, using for control and pinning situations, 118–123
Lift and jerk (or trip) finish-off, 20
Limp arm, 140, 141–142, 159
Lines of defense, 124
Long sit-out, 68
Lower body takedown maneuvers, 14–19
　double-leg, 14–17
　single-leg, 17–18

Mat drills, 160–161
Match instructions, 165–166
Military press, 162

Navy ride, 114
Near side cradle, 110–111
Neck exercise, 164
Neutral position (skill improvement) drills, 157–158
Ninety-second shooting drill, 158
Noncontact set-up, 9

Offensive moves (from the bottom), 62–89
　base positions, 62–64
　escapes, 64–78
　reversals, 79–90
180-degree turn, 128–129
One-on-one and rear crotch ride, 96–98
Outside leg stand-up, 67
Outside tripod, 69–70
Over-and-under tie, 131–132
Overhooks, 76
　countering, 141
Overtie and block, 132

Pancake, 47, 130–131
Pancake and counter, 158
Penetration, 11–12
Pinning combinations, 104–118
　bar arm and hook series, 114–118
　cradles, 104–114
　half nelson, 104
　navy ride, 114
Pinning defense, 146–148
　back hooks, 148
　cradles, 146–148
　mat drills, 160–161
Posture row, 164
Practice, 152
　daily schedule, 153–154
　weekly schedule, 154–155
Prone position, counters from, 143
Pulley chains, 164

INDEX

Quarter nelson, 130

Recradle, 147–148
Referee's position, 62–64
Reverse bodylock, 126
Reverse winglock, 99–101
Reversals (offensive moves from the bottom), 79–90
   bridge roll, 82–90
   shoulder roll, 79–80
   situation roll, 80–82
   standing shoulder roll, 82
   wing roll, 82
Riding maneuvers, 92–104
   ankle checks, 94–95
   bulldog ride, 95–96
   hammerlock, 103–104
   head lever, 98–99
   inside crotch pry and near-arm chop, 94
   one-on-one and rear crotch ride, 96–98
   reverse winglock, 99–101
   tight waist and near-arm control at wrist, 101–102
   tight waist ride, 93
   Turk ride, 102
Rolls, counters against, 139
Russian tie-up, 50–54, 132

Scoot away, 72
Set-up, 9
   contact, 158
   noncontact, 158
Shoot, defend, shoot, 158
Short sit-out, 138
Short sit series, 68–69
Shoulder press, 163
Shoulder rolls, 79–80, 158–159
   cutting off, 139
Shrug, 30
Side roll, 141

Single-leg takedown, 17–18
Sit-out, countering, 138–139
Sit-out and head check, 78
Sit and push back, 69
Situation roll, 80–82
Sit-ups, 164
Six-foot penetration, 12
Skill development, 152
Skill improvement drills, 157–161
   bottom, 158–159
   neutral position, 157–158
   top, 160
Snap down, 59
Spinning, 160
Stance, 5–8
Standing shoulder roll, 82
Stand-ups, 159
   countering, 132–137
Stepping over, 126
Straight cradle, 107–108
Straight pulls, 42
Swing set, 42–44
Switch, countering, 139–140
Switch, reswitch, 161

Takedowns, 5–61
   components of, 5
   finish-off, 14
   from kneeling-facing, 61
   lower body, 14–19
   penetration, 11–12
   set-up, 9
   stance, 5–8
   upper body, 20–30
   upper-lower body (combined maneuvers), 31–60
Three-point base position, 62–64
Throw-by, 60
Tight waist, 93, 140
   and near-arm control at the wrist, 101–102
Toe raises, 163

Top (skill improvement) drills, 160
Top offense, defensing, 140–146
Tri-extension, 164
Turk cradle, 114
Turk ride, 102, 120–121
   countering, 145–146
Twenty-second switch drill, 160
Two-arm curl, 162
Two-arm reverse curl, 162
Two-arm wrist curl, 162
Two-on-one, 50
   with a front trip, 136

Underhook, 132
Underhook to duck under, 42
Underhook series, 38–41
Upper body attacks, countering, 131–132
Upper body drill, 158
Upper body takedown maneuvers, 20–23
   arm drags, 26–28
   cross duck under, 25
   duck under, 20
   front pressure trip, 22–23
   shrug, 30
Upper-lower body takedown maneuvers, combined, 31–60
   barrel roll, 47–48, 58
   bear hug, 42
   cross elbow and knee snatch, 31
   crunch, 50
   dump, 50
   head spear to knee snatch, 32–33
   heel pick, 42
   high-crotch takedown, 34–37
   pancake, 47
   Russian tie-up, 50–54
   snap down, 59
   straight pulls, 42
   swing set, 42–44
   throw-by, 60
   two-on-one, 50
   underhook series, 38–41
   underhook to duck under, 42
Upright roll, 163

Waistlock and bump, 126
Weight classification, 4
Weight-training exercises, 162–164
   conventional, 162–163
   Universal program, 163–164
Wing roll, 82
Wrestler's grip, 108
Wrestling:
   general information, 3–4
   glossary of terms, 167–171
   how to become a good wrestler, 149–156
   introduction to, xi